The Student Life Ha

Palgrave Study Guides

Palgrave Study Guides: Literature
General Editors: John Peck and Martin Coyle

The Student Life Handbook

Christine Fanthome

macmillan

First published 2005 by
PALGRAVE MACMILLAN
Houndmills, Basingstoke, Hampshire RG21 6XS and
175 Fifth Avenue, New York, N.Y. 10010
Companies and representatives throughout the world

PALGRAVE MACMILLAN is the global academic imprint of the Palgrave Macmillan division of St. Martin's Press, LLC and of Palgrave Macmillan Ltd. Macmillan® is a registered trademark in the United States, United Kingdom and other countries. Palgrave is a registered trademark in the European Union and other countries.

ISBN-13: 978 1–4039–4897–7
ISBN-10: 1–4039–4897–6

This book is printed on paper suitable for recycling and made from fully managed and sustained forest sources.

A catalogue record for this book is available from the British Library.

10 9 8 7 6 5 4 3 2 1
14 13 12 11 10 09 08 07 06 05

Printed and bound in Great Britain by
Antony Rowe Ltd, Chippenham, Wiltshire

For
Alexei, Ivan and Tatiana
Have fun!

Contents

Preface

Have you thought about the active steps you can take to ensure that your time at university is both fun and productive? *The Student Life Handbook* is a comprehensive guide that looks at every aspect of student life from the perspective of new undergraduates. It outlines what to expect, offers information and practical advice on how to meet the challenges, and suggests strategies to ease lifestyle problems and optimise opportunities and resources. Drawing on the experiences of over 160 students from all over the United Kingdom, this book presents an extensive exposition of contemporary student life. By demystifying university culture and the day-to-day issues arising from living away from home, this book will point out how you can reap the greatest possible benefit and enjoyment from your time at university.

In recent years there have been significant reforms within higher education: government initiatives have supported and encouraged widening participation with the aim of encouraging more students to apply to universities than ever before; tuition fees are in place and variable tuition fees will be introduced in 2006, and the student loan system is now well established. Chapter 1 presents an overview of higher education, and, taking into consideration the latest statistics and reports on graduate destinations and salaries, assesses the benefits of going to university. This chapter will help you understand the current debates about higher education, and enable you to form your own conclusions.

From this point onwards the book adopts a more practical approach, identifying the key components of student life, and offering advice and information on a wide variety of topics. Each chapter is complemented by a selection of quotations from students who share their impressions and experiences. Lifestyle choices are important and can determine whether or not the university experience is a fulfilling one. With this in mind Chapter 2 focuses on common expectations, and the considerations that should be taken into account not only when choosing a university and a course, but also when making lifestyle decisions. For many students, attending university means leaving home for the first time, and this can generate added pressure if the person concerned is unprepared. Taking control of your domestic life frees up more time for study and other activities, so Chapter 3 looks at how you can prepare for independent living, what you might wish to take to university and how to cope with basic domestic tasks.

Chapters 4–8 cover various aspects of life at university. Chapter 4 emphasises the importance of maintaining a good social life in parallel with university study, and highlights the opportunities available. It points out what freshers should expect in the first few weeks and describes some typical freshers' events. It also looks at problems that may arise in the early days at university in terms of new and ongoing friendships and possible feelings of social exclusion and isolation, together with the dilemmas of integrating home commitments into undergraduate life. Chapter 5 concentrates on financial matters. You will need to be able to devise and work to a simple budget and this chapter illustrates how to go about it. It outlines key areas of expenditure and provides detailed information on student loans and student support. It examines the options for borrowing money, evaluates the advantages and disadvantages of taking paid employment whilst studying and suggests ways to economise.

Finding somewhere to live can be very daunting, especially if you are leaving home for the first time. Chapter 6 looks at the pros and cons of accommodation choices, including living in hall, renting a room with a family, and flat-sharing. It offers advice on how to find accommodation, explains the financial and legal implications of the various options, and suggests how to find compatible housemates. It also points out the most common causes of domestic tension.

Chapter 7 provides a brief introduction to university study, focusing particularly on lectures, seminars, group projects and tutorials. This chapter points out the differences between university and sixth form or college study and identifies the problems that undergraduates may encounter. There is a great deal more freedom at university than at school in terms of structuring your working schedule. With an efficient working strategy you will be able to integrate your social life with your work and gain the maximum enjoyment from each. However, certain skills are essential, especially those connected with organisation and time management. This chapter highlights skills that can be particularly useful and shows how they can be maximised to ensure a smooth path through university study. It also includes a section on the value of the university library, explaining how to deal with reading lists, and identifying how to make efficient use of library and other university resources such as IT.

It is very important to maintain your physical well-being and security whilst at university, and Chapter 8 outlines what to do if you need medical or dental treatment. It also explains how you can enhance your personal safety and safeguard your possessions. It emphasises the need for a balanced, nutritious diet, and includes fundamental facts about nutrition. It also focuses on dealing with the new social freedoms that accompany independent living, looking at issues such as balancing work and leisure, and the specific problems that may arise from exposure to drugs and alcohol.

Not all students leave school and attend university; not all live away from home; not all are UK students; some have special requirements. Chapter 9 looks at student sub-groups such as those with disabilities; students from overseas; mature students and those engaged in distance learning. Reading about other people's experiences is a good way of finding out about the range of options available to students, common mistakes, and tried and tested tips. It also brings home the fact that student life is multifaceted, with no two individuals sharing an identical experience. Chapter 10 offers a range of case studies to illustrate this. The book concludes with a series of useful checklists and summaries in Chapter 11, which draw together the key points from each chapter. An appendix provides a comprehensive list of useful websites and telephone numbers.

In the course of writing *The Student Life Handbook* I received help and support from a number of sources, and I should like to take this opportunity to thank those concerned. First, to all my colleagues within the academic community who introduced me to their students: Sue Addinell; Dr Sara Bragg; Professor Andrew Crisell; Dr Liesbeth de Block; Sara Doherty; Sue Dooks; Dr Lois Drawmer; Dr Ilya Eigenbrot; Jacky Fairfax; Sarah Glossop; Dr Judy Hemingway; Nicola Macleod; Tom Nicholls; Dr Helen Nicholson; Karin O'Neill; Beverley Poling; Merrilyn Viney and Dr Glyn White. Second, to all the organisations who made their data available and answered queries: AGR; DELNI; DfES; DH; HESA; ImechE; Nightline; NUS; OCD-UK; SAAS; Shelter; SKILL, UCAS and the Welsh Assembly Government. Third, and most important of all, to the students from universities around the country who have been so enthusiastic about contributing to the book and sharing their unique insights. Over 160 students from the following institutions were involved in this project: Bristol University; Brunel University; Buckinghamshire Chilterns University College; Cambridge University (St Edmund's College); Cardiff University; University of Central Lancashire; City and Islington College; Dr Challoner's Grammar School; Dr Challoner's High School; Edinburgh University; Greenwich University; Hertfordshire University; Kingston University; Lincoln University; Liverpool University; London University (Imperial College, Institute of Education, King's College and Royal Holloway); The Open University; Oxford University (Hertford College); Queen Margaret University College; St Mary's College (Twickenham); Stirling University; University of Surrey Roehampton; and Sussex University. All student names have been changed throughout the book to protect each individual's identity.

Special thanks are due to David Malcolm from the NUS for reading the first draft and offering helpful and productive suggestions. Finally, I should like to thank my publisher Suzannah Burywood, my husband Rudolph Kalveks, and my children, Alexei, Ivan and Tatiana, for supporting and encouraging me while I was researching and writing this book.

C.F.

List of Abbreviations

AGR	Association of Graduate Recruiters
BNF	British Nutrition Foundation
CCCS	Consumer Credit Counselling Service
DELNI	Department of Employment and Learning (Northern Ireland)
DfES	Department for Education and Skills
DLHE	Destination of Leavers from Higher Education
DRC	Disability Rights Commission
DSA	Disabled Students' Allowance
EEA	European Economic Area
HECSU	Higher Education Careers Services Unit
HEPI	Higher Education Policy Institute
HESA	Higher Education Statistics Agency
HHSRS	Housing Health and Safety Rating System
HMO	Housing in Multiple Occupation
ISIC	International Student Identity Card
MORI	Market and Opinion Research International
NASES	National Association of Student Employment Services
NCWE	National Council for Work Experience
OFFA	Office for Fair Access
QAA	Quality Assurance Agency
SAAS	Student Awards Agency for Scotland
SLC	Student Loans Company
UCAS	University and Colleges Admission Service
UKCOSA	United Kingdom Council for Overseas Student Affairs (now known as the Council for International Education)

1 Behind the Headlines – Debates about Higher Education

This chapter will look at some of the key issues in higher education and what they mean for you. Specifically it will:

- give an overview of current government thinking and objectives
- comment on student life in the twenty-first century
- assess the benefits of going to university
- provide information on a number of relevant issues such as graduate destinations, graduate salaries and university drop-out rates

▶ A time of change

The purpose of this chapter is to explain the debates surrounding higher education so that you can come to your own conclusions and take the course of action that is best for you. In recent years, student life has undergone many changes, and more are on the horizon. The maintenance grant system has been phased out and replaced by repayable student loans with financial support for low-income applicants; students now pay tuition fees, and variable top-up fees (an increase in fees up to a maximum of £3000, depending on the course), commence in 2006. In addition, the Government's policy of widening participation has sought to raise the percentage of young people embarking upon higher education courses to 50 per cent.

▶ Government reforms

This section looks at Government reforms in terms of student finance. It explains the rationale behind the changes and points out what this will mean to you, especially in terms of the costs associated with going to university.

Why the Government introduced changes

Prior to its election in 1997, and against a backdrop of widespread complaints from universities about long-standing underinvestment and funding problems, Labour declared a commitment to reforming student finance and support, and to widening access to higher education. It argued that students should contribute towards higher education costs because later on they would reap the benefits in terms of career opportunities and financial rewards. It pledged to put a loan system in place and offer graduates the opportunity to borrow money to finance their living costs whilst at university and pay the loan back over a long period of time once their earnings had reached a sufficient level. It also planned extra support for low-income students, to enable all candidates reaching the required standard, regardless of class or background, to go on to higher education.

Tuition fees – the Government's rationale

As a result of the new Teaching and Higher Education Act 1998, students starting higher education degrees were required to contribute to tuition fees of up to £1000 per year, although those qualifying as lower income households had part or all of this sum paid. (This figure then rose with inflation each year.) There then followed a period of debate about whether or not to raise the tuition fee for certain courses, which culminated in the decision to introduce variable top-up fees of up to £3000 a year from 2006. The Government's argument for the introduction of tuition fees in 1998 and variable top-up fees in 2006 was that the money generated, together with government funding, would counter recent underinvestment and bring UK spending on higher education in line with other countries, whereas previously the UK had lagged behind. This was confirmed in the DfES (Department for Education and Skills) report *Higher Education Funding – International Comparisons*, which noted that in 2000 UK spending per student in tertiary education, at $9657, was 'below the OECD[1] mean average and under half of what the US spent ($20,358)'.[2] In addition to the extra income generated from top-up fees, the Government pledged to increase spending from £7.5 billion a year to just under £10 billion a year between 2002/3 and 2005/6. Defending his reforms, the Prime Minister, Tony Blair, confirmed that the problems brought on by previous underfunding needed to be redressed, particularly in view of the anticipated expansion in student numbers by 2010:

> Why is it necessary to do this? It is necessary because there's been a 36 per cent fall in funding per student in the 8 years prior to us coming to office. It is necessary because university places are being expanded. We

are now at 43 per cent of under 30's in university, but that is projected to rise. There's a misunderstanding here sometimes. People say we have set some sort of arbitrary target. The reason we have an aim of 50 per cent is that it is actually projected that it will rise to 50 per cent by 2010 in line with both rising school standards and employer demands, and it is necessary to make these changes also because even with this expansion we are still getting far too low participation rates from the poorest families.[3]

Controversy surrounding tuition fees

However, the reforms were controversial, particularly the issue of variable top-up fees, which has given rise to several concerns. One view is that top-up fees may deter poorer students despite student support packages for those on the lowest incomes.[4] It is felt that the situation may be particularly difficult for those from low-income households who are nevertheless just above the level required to qualify for extra support. Moreover, not all parents who are considered by the authorities to be capable of helping their children with their university expenses, actually do so. As a result, certain individuals may be burdened with a higher level of debt than those from similar backgrounds whose parents elect to make a financial contribution. Middle-income students who do not receive a grant and yet who are not largely funded by their parents are likely to graduate with a larger student loan debt than those who either receive the grant or who are given money by their parents.

Also, it is argued that students who need to take on paid work throughout their undergraduate years, and who are therefore not able to devote time to voluntary work or other interests that enhance their CVs (curriculum vitae), are then at a disadvantage after they graduate when the time comes to seek a job. Under the present system, the level of debt that an individual has on graduation is partially determined by the financial circumstances of his or her family when the higher education course commenced, and this is seen by some as a serious flaw in the current arrangements. There are also fears that the majority of universities will charge the top rate of £3000 in order to make ends meet, so the fees will not actually be as 'variable' as was anticipated.[5]

What will happen in the future?

There are concerns that the £3000 ceiling will need to be raised still further because, despite top-up fees, there remains a considerable shortfall. A recent report by Oxford University confirms that this sum is not considered adequate:

Recurrent costs exceed revenues because nearly all of the University's core activities lose money. Educating the average undergraduate has been estimated to cost £18,600 per annum as against a total income of £9,500 ... The introduction of variable fees for home/EU undergraduates will make only a small dent in the loss per student.[6]

Oxford's plans to 'gradually decrease undergraduate numbers over a five-year period'[7] whilst simultaneously to 'implement a vigorous programme of international recruitment'[8] have led to vociferous accusations in the press that home students, who pay considerably lower fees than overseas students, will be disadvantaged as universities are forced to seek ways of generating more income. The *Guardian*, for example, reported that Oxford 'proposed slashing the number of places for British undergraduates in favour of those from abroad as part of a package of radical measures to maintain its standing in the international "super league" of universities',[9] whilst the *Daily Mail* stated that 'the proposals faced growing backlash ... from academics, politicians and the National Union of Students, who said foreign undergraduates should not simply be regarded as "pound signs"'.[10]

The introduction of variable fees has opened up a market in higher education: each institution will need to determine what it is able to charge for individual courses whilst still being able to attract students in sufficient numbers for its courses to be viable. Students, as consumers, are likely to 'shop around' for the best deals and this will affect what is on offer. Universities will have difficult choices to make: some may close or downsize courses, either because student interest is not sufficient, or because they involve equipment and resources that render the course cost inefficient. This explanation accounts for some of the recent closures of science courses, as noted in the press, such as the decision by Exeter not to continue to offer chemistry and the science cuts implemented by Keele and Newcastle.[11]

Whereas, at present, students who pay all or part of their tuition fees must make an up-front payment, from 2006 students will be able to increase their loan to take tuition fees into account, which means that students who cannot find the capital at the outset will no longer find this an obstacle to pursuing a higher education course. The details of how to apply for a loan, the amount of money that can be borrowed, the student support available, repayment arrangements and so on are covered in detail in Chapter 5.

Student debt

As students are responsible for paying their tuition fees and also for supporting themselves throughout their time at university, usually by taking out a repayable loan, most now graduate with considerable debts. However, recent research indicates that whilst students are naturally concerned about this, they are not overwhelmed by it. Nicholas Porter, Chief Executive Officer of UNITE, the UK's largest provider of student accommodation services, commenting on a Student Experience Report involving over 1000 students, (commissioned by UNITE and carried out by MORI), states:

> This generation of students is perhaps the first to accept and feel at ease with the fact that they will need to borrow to study and possibly work during term time to fund basic essentials. Interestingly, while a significant proportion of students are worried about debt, they are also confident of a graduate earnings premium which will pay off their debts following graduation.[12]

The report established that students anticipate graduating with debts of around £9744. It found that 49 per cent of students are not worried about their debts whilst studying because they are confident that they will pay them off when they start working. Although 31 per cent are 'seriously worried' about their debts, this figure represents a drop of 9 per cent from the number of students expressing this view in a comparable earlier survey, undertaken a year before.

As student loans are a relatively new phenomenon in the UK, the long-term effects are not known. It is not yet possible to identify and estimate the exact nature of any secondary effects of student debt: for example, whether it will influence the average number of years taken for graduates to embark upon home ownership. The potential future problems have not escaped the NUS (National Union of Students), and their president, Kat Fletcher, has criticised the Government for following the line that being in debt is inevitable and acceptable. She observes:

> This comes from ministers and politicians who enjoyed full grants and benefits and are reaping the debt-free rewards by owning their own house(s) and providing for their own children and family. Such a life will be out of the question for the next generation of graduates, who will face the burden of years of debt repayments reaching tens of thousands of pounds.[13]

It is also too early to say whether or not there will be a significant increase in the numbers of students who will seek ways of cutting costs or supplementing their income, such as by living at home throughout their undergraduate years or by opting for distance learning or sandwich courses. Certainly, the number of students under the age of 24 enrolling with the Open University has tripled since 1998 and now represents one in ten undergraduates, which is an indication that some individuals have decided to explore alternatives to 'conventional' university courses. It is likely that changing market conditions will produce new trends, but it will take some time before the nature of these becomes apparent.

▶ Foundation degrees

As part of the drive to tailor higher education content to the requirements of the workplace, foundation degrees were introduced in 2001. They focus on work-based learning and are designed in conjunction with employers to ensure that students acquire the skills and experience necessary to contribute immediately within a workplace environment. There are no specified entry requirements as the candidate's employment experience is taken into account. A full-time course takes two years, and a part-time course takes approximately three to four years, after which the individual may go on to take a full honours degree with a further 12 to 15 months' full-time study, or the part-time equivalent. For students who want to acquire practical experience and training that is immediately relevant in the workplace, foundation degrees may be a good choice. (See Conor's experience in Chapter 10).

Widening participation – research and suggestions

The Government has expressed a strong commitment to widening participation in higher education, noting in its White Paper, *The Future of Higher Education*, that disadvantaged groups are under-represented in higher education, and advocating fair access because 'education is the best and most reliable route out of poverty and disadvantage'.[14] With this in mind the Aimhigher initiative was launched to raise aspirations amongst disadvantaged groups and to forge better links between schools, colleges and universities through outreach programmes, including summer schools. The Paper also pledged more support for students from low-income households, more guidance for universities to ensure fair and open admissions policies, better benchmark data for institutions to enable self-monitoring of progress in widening participation initiatives and a reform of the access premium. Data released by HESA (Higher Education Statistics Agency) showed that '13.3 per cent of young entrants to full-time degree courses came from low participation neighbourhoods in 2002/03' and '28.4 per cent' in the same year 'came from the lowest four [of seven] socio-economic groups'.[15]

Following publication of the White Paper, the Government instigated several specialist reports to analyse the specific problems and make recommendations. These included the House of Commons Education and Skills Committee, which remarked that 'access should depend on academic ability', but that 'the priority for widening participation must be action in schools', as 'considerable effort is required to raise the aspiration and achievement of pupils from poorer backgrounds. It is only by doing this that the proportion of those from the lower socio-economic groups entering higher education is likely to increase.'[16]

The Government proposals with regards to the Office for Fair Access (OFFA) were detailed in *Widening Participation in Higher Education*.[17] This noted that one in four working-class students with eight good GCSE passes did not undertake higher education, and advocated that universities should do more to encourage applications from sections of the community currently under-represented in higher education. The document outlined what could be done to improve the current situation. Subsequently, a steering group, chaired by Professor Steven Schwartz, was set up to identify good practice in admissions.[18] The final report noted that admissions processes were 'generally fair' but that there was 'room for improvement'. Although the steering group declared that it did 'not want to bias admissions in favour of applicants from certain backgrounds or schools', it urged institutions to think more laterally when assessing candidates for admission:

> It is not the task of higher education admissions to compensate for educational or social disadvantage. But identifying latent talent and potential, which may not fully be demonstrated by examination results, is a legitimate aim for universities and colleges to seek to recruit the best possible students regardless of backgrounds.[19]

Controversy surrounding widening participation policies

The widening participation initiative has proved controversial and has provoked intense media coverage and debate. On the one hand, it is seen as making higher education more accessible to disadvantaged groups but, on the other hand, it is perceived as social engineering that discriminates against certain candidates, such as those from public schools or selective grammar schools. The rationale behind this latter accusation is based on two main observations. The first is that universities opting to charge £3000 tuition fees must prove to OFFA that they are taking steps to widen access in order to receive the Access Agreement (and related finance) that they require to proceed. However, it should be noted that the requirements relate to encouraging applications rather than directing admissions policy, and that the latter remains a matter for each individual institution.

The second is that some universities have announced that they will not necessarily make offers on the basis of examination grades, and this has been interpreted as discriminating against applicants with good results from independent or grammar schools. There has been abundant press coverage on this: 'Bristol history department has been praised by the higher education minister, Margaret Hodge, for accepting young people with low A-level results whom it considers to have the potential to do well.'[20] 'Edinburgh University said academic qualifications were not the only way of judging how students would perform at degree level. . . . Admissions tutors will be expected to look at the "context" in which candidates achieved their A-level and Scottish Highers grades, the university said.'[21] Along similar lines, some universities have partnership schemes with local schools. Newcastle University has been involved in such a scheme since 2000. Specific students are targeted because of financial or family circumstances and a proportion of them are then offered places at the university despite having lower A-level grades than some other applicants. Newcastle's scheme started with 40 students, rising to 340 students in 2002. Data indicate that 'students accepted with lower A-level offers from local schools are performing as well as their better-qualified peers', with 4.2 per cent failing or resitting their exams at the end of the first year compared to an average of 8.5 per cent for the university as a whole.[22] The reasoning behind these and other compara-ble admissions decisions relates to the findings of a study by the Higher Education Policy Institute, which concluded that:

> . . . generally A-levels are a reasonable pointer. But A-levels do not tell the whole story. For example, it is now well established that pupils from inde-pendent schools do less well in university than pupils from state schools with similar A-level grades, as is shown [refers to a specific chart in the report]. This is not an attack on A-levels. A-levels remain an extremely effective way of identifying academic potential, and we would be foolish to undermine them in any way. But it is clear too that universities need to use a certain amount of discretion in making their judgements.[23]

It is not just the selection criteria that have come under scrutiny, but also the figure of 50 per cent of students going on to higher education which has sparked controversy. Whereas some welcome a larger proportion of students continuing their education after the sixth form or college, others believe that the figure is too high; that universities will lower standards in order to fill places and that the higher education route may not be appropriate for this number of individuals.

Earlier in this chapter I quoted from a Prime Minister's Press Conference in which Tony Blair spoke of the 50 per cent figure as emerging naturally as a result of 'rising school standards and employer demands'.[24] The Government also answers its critics by pointing to international comparisons which indicate that the UK higher education participation rate is below the average of the OECD (Organisation for Economic Co-operation and Development) countries. A DfES document cites the average participation rate as being 47 per cent and the UK rate as being 45 per cent. It notes that several countries have considerably higher participation rates than the UK, such as New Zealand (76 per cent), Finland (72 per cent), Poland (67 per cent) Australia (65 per cent), Iceland (61 per cent), and the Netherlands (54 per cent).[25]

Drop-out rates
However, opponents of a 50 per cent participation rate cite lowering standards and a rise in university drop-out rates as consequences of encouraging greater numbers to go on to higher education. Sue Fishburn, the Headmistress of Leeds Girls' High School, whilst supportive of a partnership scheme at Leeds University, is quoted in the press as having concerns about the trend: 'The problem the universities have is trying to level the playing field. They shouldn't be doing remedial teaching. This Government is trying to put right failures at secondary school level by putting it in the universities' hands.' (The newspaper notes that Ms Fishburn pointed out that only about half of children were getting the minimum qualifications of five A to C grades at GCSE.) She goes on to comment: 'Where on earth are they coming from saying 50 per cent can get a degree?'[26] Along similar lines, Patricia O'Brien, the Head of Business at IT at Edinburgh's Telford College, is quoted as follows: 'Students who would have gone to colleges are increasingly being accepted at new universities but are then dropping out. They are being lured on to courses not appropriate for them.'[27] Bahram Bekhradnia, director of the Higher Education Policy Institute, states: 'We have to accept that the government policy on widening access, if it means admitting more students with less traditional qualifications, will inevitably lead to higher drop-out rates.'[28]

In September 2004, HESA published its performance indicators for 2002/03, which projected a 14.1 per cent drop-out rate for higher education students.[29] Some newspapers published 'drop-out league tables' which indicated that certain institutions had non-completion rates in excess of 25 per cent.[30] There was additional comment that some universities with poor completion rates were changing their assessment criteria in a bid to reduce drop-out rates:

> The University of Middlesex has become the first institution to abolish exams for its first-year students. . . . A *Guardian* table rates Middlesex's

drop-out rate at 25 per cent and this high figure has led to some specula-
tion that the abolishment of exams is a means to reduce it. But this has
been vehemently denied by the university, which has stressed that it
considers coursework the best way to 'facilitate learning'.[31]

The DfES's response to criticism is to state that the UK has 'one of the lowest
university drop-out rates in the OECD so our universities are generally good
at finding the right students for the right courses'.[32]

Clearly, a decrease in drop-outs would benefit both universities and
students, and arguably the way forward is for all potential students to have a
clearer idea of what to expect prior to commencing higher education. It is
perhaps unsurprising that students who are the first in their family to go to
university may be less clear about what to expect and may therefore experience more problems. This situation is being redressed to an extent with the
provision of outreach work in sixth forms, summer schools, open days and
'taster' days. Potential university students can help themselves further by
exploring the web pages of their chosen institute, meeting current students,
and reading books such as this one which outline the key aspects of life as a
higher education student and give pointers for further information or specific
areas of concern.

▶ Student life in the twenty-first century

You may find it useful to consider some of the statistics available that give an
indication of what life is like for today's students. As I have mentioned previously in this chapter, changes to higher education financing, and most
particularly the onus on the student to pay tuition fees and cost-of-living
expenses, have meant that living with a growing debt has become the norm
for today's undergraduates. Taking on paid employment in parallel with
university study is also commonplace, and a recent report on student life
estimates that 42 per cent of students are in this position, with the majority
of them undertaking catering, retail or bar work. It was found that on
average students work 14.5 hours per week and are paid approximately £86,
but 14 per cent work over 20 hours per week.[33] The same report notes that
79 per cent are more or less able to keep up with bills and credit commitments. The survey finds that 77 per cent of students in debt owe money as
the result of a student loan; 36 per cent have a bank overdraft; 17 per cent
owe money to a credit card company and 11 per cent owe money to their
parents. Two per cent of students in the survey stated that they had fallen
behind with bills and were in a serious financial situation.

In terms of outlook, the UNITE/MORI report finds that 88 per cent of students are happy with their lives. Although about 33 per cent purchase more alcohol than the number of units recommended by the Department of Health, they are generally very health aware, caring about health and fitness (71 per cent), knowledgeable about the dangers of binge drinking (59 per cent) and appreciative of the risks of taking drugs.

The report does show a fall in the time spent campaigning on current issues, such as the environment. Nicholas Porter, Chief Executive officer of UNITE, attributes this to lack of time caused by the necessity to combine paid work with studying. My own research for this book, which involved contact with over 160 students from universities all over the country, concurs with the above findings. Today's students are very busy juggling employment and study commitments. They are well aware of the financial restrictions imposed by their situation and, generally, most are able to navigate their way through it and find solutions, albeit after a shaky start in some cases. However, it is apparent that several students have sought solutions in order to avoid further debt, for example by opting for distance learning, by working in their gap year and consciously saving all their earnings for their university years, or by choosing to live at home whilst studying. It will be interesting to observe if new trends emerge in the aftermath of the 2006 academic year and the proposed changes.

▶ Benefits of higher education – finding work and earning more

In recent years, numbers of applications to university have increased steadily. UCAS data reveal a rise from 339,747 accepted applicants in 2000 to 374,307 in 2003. A recent report notes that 70 per cent of students attend university primarily in order to gain a qualification.[34] This is perhaps unsurprising in view of the statistical evidence from a variety of sources that indicates higher education improves both an individual's chance of finding employment and also the likelihood of achieving a higher salary.

Graduate salaries
You will no doubt be pleased to learn that research published in 2004 by the Association of Graduate Recruiters (AGR), offered good news for graduates in that it indicated both an increase in the number of graduate vacancies for the first time in four years, and an increase in graduate salaries.[35] The report noted that the median starting salaries had reached £21,000, which represented an increase of 3.4 per cent on the previous year; 42 per cent of AGR

members increased their graduate starting salaries by more than 2.5 per cent in 2004; and 39 per cent did not make changes. The highest graduate starting salaries were found in London and the south-east (£25,000 and £21,500 respectively) and the lowest were in Scotland (£18,500) and Northern Ireland (£18,000).[36] The highest starting salaries were to be found in the investment banking sector (£35,000), consulting firms (£28,500) and law firms (£28,000).

The research for this report was carried out by High Fliers Research and based on the responses of AGR members. It should be noted that AGR membership tends to include the largest graduate recruiters from both the private and the public sectors and, as such, the salaries quoted are arguably higher than the figures for graduate starting salaries as a whole. Indeed, HESA's report on the destinations of graduate leavers 2002/2003 puts the median salary at £17,000. *Graduate Market Trends*, a quarterly publication produced by Graduate Prospects (the trading subsidiary of the charity HECSU), reveals that predictions for 2005 indicate an average graduate salary of £21,997. The January 2005 report reveals that graduate salaries tend to range from £13,242 to £36,000, but that approximately 25 per cent will start above £25,000 and above.[37] These figures are based on vacancies advertised in Prospects Directory, which features larger firms and specific areas of recruitment. As such the salaries offered are likely to be higher than the figures relating to *all* graduates.

The data from Prospects Directory revealed other interesting information, such as the fact that 75.8 per cent of all vacancies did not require a specific subject discipline. This is in keeping with the notion that employers appreciate the value of underlying skills acquired through higher education, such as the ability to organise, communicate and solve problems.

Graduate destinations

The Higher Education Statistics Agency (HESA) publishes data on the destinations of leavers from higher education and other related matters on its website www.hesa.ac.uk. The data relating to leavers from 2002/2003 reveals that of the 248,000 individuals who completed the survey, 72.7 per cent had found employment and 6.2 per cent were assumed to be unemployed.[38]

The same report noted that employment rates varied according to degree subject, with the highest being medicine and dentistry (91.8 per cent), subjects allied to medicine (85.6 per cent) and education (85.1 per cent). The lowest employment rates were for historical and philosophical studies (61.9 per cent), physical sciences (58.9 per cent) and law (49.9 per cent). However, these figures do not tell the whole story because some leavers in some subjects go on to undertake further study before taking up employment. The highest percentage of leavers assumed to be unemployed were computer science graduates (12.5 per cent) and the least likely to be unemployed were medicine and dentistry leavers (0.2 per cent).

A successful career immediately as undergraduate studies come to an end cannot, however, be guaranteed, and as more graduates enter the employment market, some find themselves in 'non-graduate' types of job. Based on its interpretation of recent HESA data, Matthew Taylor, the *Guardian* education correspondent, states: 'More than a third of students who start work when they finish their degree end up in non-graduate jobs, from stacking shelves to answering phones in call centres.'[39] In the same report, James Knight, president of NUS Wales, explains that: 'Many students are so crippled by debt at the end of their course that they are forced to take whatever work they can get to keep their head above water.' Given that most students are motivated to embark upon higher education courses because they believe this will enhance their career prospects, these observations are worrying.

Clearly, many employers, not just those who require specialist graduate knowledge from job applicants, are drawn towards graduate candidates because of the useful 'soft' skills they tend to possess. Attendance at university generally means that the individual will have acquired self-learning experience, together with time-management, communication and organisational skills. It also implies commitment, ambition and determination, all of which are qualities that are attractive to employers. Individuals should not be deterred from going on to higher education as the likelihood is that if employers wish and are able to find graduates to fill some of the more junior vacancies, young people without higher education experience will find it even more difficult to reach the first rung of the employment ladder. There is also an argument that in the early days of an individual's career, workplace experience is essential in establishing a portfolio of skills that can be used later for career advancement.

Indeed, research has shown that the situation immediately after graduation does not represent the long-term picture. A new report, *Seven Years On: Graduate Careers in a Changing Labour Market*,[40] which looks at employment issues relating to a group of 4500 students from 38 UK higher education institutions who graduated in 1995, reveals some optimistic findings. Although immediately after graduation 43 per cent were in non-graduate jobs, seven years later 90 per cent were in graduate jobs, with 75 per cent in jobs that related to their long-term career plans. Moreover, the report found that the range of jobs available to today's graduates is wider than in the past, that higher education expansion has not led to fewer opportunities for graduates, and that employers are still prepared to pay more for graduates. Commenting on the findings, the authors note:

The research shows the value of taking a long-term perspective. It is clear that graduate career paths evolve slowly: some graduates take five years or longer to settle into their careers; for some it involves further study, for others the process of assimilation into the labour market involves false starts or a rethink about their early career choices.

This is also borne out by the findings of *What Do Graduates Do? 2005*. This is a report produced by Graduate Prospects, the Association of Graduate Careers Advisory Services (AGCAS), and UCAS (the Universities and Colleges Admissions Service), based on the HESA First Destination survey. Aiming to analyse the potential outcomes of a range of degree subjects, the 2005 report notes that the appeal of teaching is reflected in the destinations of graduates of several subjects including maths and English. One in six maths graduates went on to teach or to take a postgraduate maths qualification, and one in six English graduates entered teaching. The report also shows that vocational degrees continued to provide a sound basis for future employment, with civil engineering degrees proving particularly successful: 72.3 per cent of civil engineering graduates found employment in the UK or abroad. Although 11.3 per cent of graduates took secretarial or clerical positions, the report also shows that many students (58 per cent) tended not to focus seriously on job hunting until after they graduated, so may not immediately have settled into their chosen career. Mike Hill, chief executive of Graduate Prospects, notes:

> ... graduates from some degrees take longer than others to decide on their long-term futures, often taking more administrative positions while they consider their options; others use such positions as footholds into companies for which they would like to work. The idea that all graduates should sail from university into high paid graduate jobs within weeks of graduation is a myth and always has been.[41]

A higher education qualification does not guarantee employment, but it provides you with knowledge and skills that can then be utilised in the workplace, with the content of some degree subjects having a closer relationship to specific jobs than others. Graduates then need to 'adapt' their skills and experience to meet the needs of the employment market in their chosen field. This is not necessarily automatic, and is likely to involve a further investment of time and effort.

It is important not to lose sight of the fact that there are many other benefits associated with higher education study than simply securing a better job and earnings. These include the valuable experience of mixing with people from all walks of life. You are likely to encounter people from a wide variety of nationalities and cultural backgrounds, which as well as broadening intellectual horizons can open up new ways of looking at the world and help you to define what you want from your future. University can also lead to travel opportunities, both through formal exchange programmes and also through informal arrangements you may wish to make with your friends for the vacations or after graduation. Your own studying will significantly increase your personal knowledge of an academic subject, but in addition you will also learn about topics outside of your specialisation through interaction with other students. University life offers the opportunity to become involved in a vast range of activities, including political campaigns and voluntary work, at either a local or national level. It also presents the chance to develop current hobbies or discover totally new ones. Student life provides an opportunity to identify how you want to live, to define what is important and to establish goals for the future. It offers an environment in which you can experiment with independent living and work out your views and preferences. The close interaction with others in the same situation usually leads to lifelong friendships and social networks. For most people, having fun and enjoying the undergraduate years are right at the top of the agenda, which is why very many graduates look back on their student years as one of the happiest and most stimulating periods of their life.

▶ Summary

The aim of this chapter was to inform you of the current issues within higher education and their implications, to enable you to identify the course of action that is right for you. It also evaluated the benefits of a university education in terms of long-term employment destinations and salary.

2 Expectations and Choices

This chapter will:

- summarise the considerations taken into account when choosing a university, subject and course
- emphasise the importance of attaching similar value to decisions relating to student life
- briefly outline the key benefits and problems associated with student life
- suggest how students can increase the likelihood of their own personal expectations being met

Making choices

Opting for university study automatically involves making a series of choices. For some people the process is relatively straightforward, particularly if they are clear about the subject they wish to study and what they want to achieve, and if they are already aware of the considerations relating to their own personal circumstances that need to be taken into account. Others may need to spend considerable time researching the courses that are best for them, and reflecting upon the lifestyle choices that best match their needs. For many, it is a lengthy process, mainly because decisions based on statistical data, or information offered in the relevant prospectus or website, may be overturned by the experience of an open day, visit to the university, or interview. For some students this chapter will represent a useful checklist to ensure that in making their choice they have taken all the necessary factors into account; for others it will offer directions through the myriad of opportunities available.

Most students opt to go to university for one or more of the following reasons:

▶ to enhance their employment and career prospects;
▶ to study a subject that they find interesting;
▶ to experience and enjoy independent living.

It therefore makes sense to reflect on your own personal views on each of these subjects and use your findings to establish the 'best' university, course and lifestyle for you. Even if you believe that you have identified the route you wish to take, it is worth thinking about the points raised in this chapter as you may find that you are clearer about your preferred course of action when you take the wider picture into account. Self-knowledge will also be extremely helpful should your situation change, for example if you become involved in the 'clearing' process or if you later decide to take a gap year. Whilst embarking upon student life is always likely to involve elements of surprise, planning and reflection can go a long way to ensure that your expectations are for the most part met, that there are no unpleasant shocks, and that you will be able to find enjoyment and fulfilment in your new situation.

▶ Finding the right academic environment

Sixth form and college students have the advantage of being able to draw on the resources of their careers office and staff when deciding on the universities and courses for which they would like to apply. However, for those who do not have access to help of this nature there is plenty of information and assistance available from web resources. The first port of call is the University and Colleges Admissions Service, UCAS. The website, www.ucas.ac.uk, offers a wealth of information about universities, courses and the application process, including how to apply online. It also contains an online test, called the Stamford Test, designed to match interests, career ambitions and skills to the most suitable higher education subjects. This was developed by occupational analysts at Cambridge University and takes ten minutes to complete online. It is particularly useful for people who are committed to the idea of university study but find the range of courses somewhat overwhelming. The Government website, www.aimhigher.ac.uk, is also good for basic information. It includes maps showing the location of each institution, a selection of 'frequently asked questions', and the relevant links for ordering a specific prospectus. Other sites include www.universityoptions. co.uk, designed by the University of Manchester in association with the *Guardian* newspaper, and www.educationguardian.co.uk, which includes annual profiles of various institutions under the 'university guide' section.

> ❝ *I did a lot of research into jobs and their requirements. Much of the top-end type of work preferred graduates, and so I've seen university as a means to an end. Within my family nobody has ever been to university and so there's a certain amount of determination in trying to be the first to go that extra step.* ❞
>
> (**Veer**, sixth-former)

The Quality Assurance Agency for higher education (QAA), undertakes reviews of the quality of higher education courses and publishes its findings on its website, www.qaa.ac.uk. These reports cover a range of aspects including the aims and objectives of the course contents; the curriculum design; student support; learning resources and the nature of assessment. In addition, various newspapers, such as *The Times* and the *Guardian*, produce annual league tables and these may be viewed on their websites. These do vary in terms of the indicators used to compile the rankings, but may include: the level of entry qualifications; percentages of degree classifications; the QAA's findings with regard to course and teaching quality; the ratio of staff to students; the financial amount allocated to student spending, for example for books and computing resources; the range of students in terms of demographic groups including minorities; the numbers of students dropping out before completing their courses; the numbers of graduates finding employment within a certain time-frame; and the type of employment found.

It is important to choose the academic framework that is right for you, so that you will cope well and enjoy studying your subject, and so that you will leave with a qualification that will help you in your chosen career. If you know what you want to do after graduation, try to find out which courses and universities are considered by the relevant employers to be most appropriate. Look at the DLHE statistics (Destination of Leavers from Higher Education) on the HESA website (www.hesa.ac.uk), relating to universities in which you are interested, as this will give you an idea of the type and level of work that recent graduates have found. These figures may also be obtained from the university department in question. Some courses are accredited by professional bodies, particularly in the vocational sphere. If this is the case it may mean that graduates of these courses who go on to take professional examinations will be exempt from certain papers.

> ❝ *I ended up deciding to attend xxx because of the good reviews it receives on its journalism course, as this is the path that I've always wished to follow. The atmosphere around the uni is good and the social life is plentiful.* ❞
>
> (**Sandy**, 1st-year undergraduate)

I felt variety was critical – where I could combine subjects rather than being restricted to just one subject.
(**Abdullah**, 1st-year undergraduate)

You should also consider the different teaching methods underpinning the courses for which you are applying, and select the ones that suit you most. Ask yourself whether you are happy to sit examinations or whether you prefer project work and dissertations. Do you like to study at your own pace or do deadlines help you to focus and get down to work? Do you prefer to study alone or in a group? Are you more interested in an academic or a vocational approach? What best motivates you? Do you like to work independently once you have been given initial instructions or is it important to you to have frequent meetings with academic staff? Try to picture yourself within the learning structure offered by each institution under consideration and ask yourself whether or not you think you would thrive within it. If you reflect on your expectations in advance, you are less likely to be disappointed.

Hopefully, having followed the steps outlined above, you will have created your own shortlist of courses and universities. You then need to obtain the prospectus from each establishment as these contain more detailed information that will help you in honing your choices. It is also a good idea to look at the relevant websites, particularly the 'frequently asked questions' sections. If possible, you should try to visit your key choices as this will enable you to get a stronger sense of whether or not you would like to study there. The University of Central Lancashire has a useful website, www.opendays.com, which notes the contact details of staff organising open days at each institution, and the web references giving the open day arrangements. Alternatively this information may be found on the website of each individual institution. You may also wish to visit a higher education fair or convention (see www.ucas.ac.uk). If you attend an open day, take the opportunity to ask any questions you may have and try to talk to some of the current students about their own experiences, as this will give you a good feel for the place. (See also the relevant checklist in Chapter 11 – *Have you decided on your course?*)

 Factors taken into account are prestige, grade requirements, distance from my home town, course structure, accommodation and living costs. Mostly I have chosen my universities on prestige and gut reaction when I walk around them.
(**Bernadette**, sixth-former)

▶ Making appropriate lifestyle choices

It is essential not only to choose the course and university that is right for you, but also to opt for an environment in which you will be happy. Lifestyle choices are important and can determine whether or not the experience is a fulfilling one. You may be flexible and find that you are not seeking one specific type of environment, but it is nevertheless a good idea to reflect on the different options and to be aware of the consequences of particular choices.

> *If I were to chose again I think I would take more notice of the atmosphere of the college and its location. Feelings you get from a place can be just as important as facts about the course.*
>
> (**John**, 2nd year-undergraduate)

> *When I was choosing where to go to uni, one of the crucial factors was whether I liked the city. I had visited xxx a few times and knew instantly that I wanted to go. The university has a lot of credibility and is a fantastic place. I liked it so much that I chose to do Scottish law over English law which added an extra year of study than if I had stayed in England. However, this didn't bother me.*
>
> (**Rakesh**, 3rd-year undergraduate)

Are you equally at ease in an inner city and in a rural location? Do you think you would find a small university friendly or claustrophobic? Would you prefer to live on a campus or would you appreciate more interaction with the outside world? What about the social life? What is the ratio of male to female students and what does the nightlife have to offer? Is it likely that you would be able to find accommodation that would suit you relatively near to the university centre, and is this affordable? Remember that property prices, and therefore rental figures, vary considerably from one part of the country to another. The repercussions of this are that people studying in comparatively expensive areas may have to live further away from the university, resulting in a wider geographical spread of student accommodation. This means that there is less likely to be a high concentration of student numbers in any one specific area and although rental costs may be lower for those living further away, travel costs will probably be higher. If you need to work whilst at university and do not wish to travel far for work, this may affect your choice, as some locations will offer more job opportunities than others. The cost of living generally may vary in different areas of the country too, with prices tending to be higher in the south. There can also be noticeable variations in climate. The distance between home and university may also be important to you. Some students prefer to live at home throughout their university years, either for financial reasons or because they see no need to go away to study. (See Catherine's experiences in Chapter 10, and Louise's comments in Chapter 6.) On the other hand, many students like to make a 'clean break' with home and deliberately opt for a university some distance away. However, if you know that you will want to visit home frequently it is worth bearing this in mind when you make your choice as travel can be time-consuming and costly. However, it is worth checking the travel options as some long-distance routes are well serviced by rail and coach links whereas other, shorter distances may actually be less convenient and involve changes and delays. Also, if you plan to take large amounts of luggage to and from university each term, and you really do need to rely on parental taxi services, you might bear this in mind when considering your options.

❛ When picking my university, I paid some attention to course outlines, league positions etc., but what was most valuable to me was the 'feel' of the campus. I was led by gut feeling, the atmosphere of the student's union, the smell of the corridors. It sounds stupid but if I hated the smell of the uni I didn't want to go there. Another big deciding factor was how well maintained the campus was. I felt that this would have an impact on my overall enjoyment of uni life.

(**Flora**, 3rd-year undergraduate)

Do you have specific requirements that some institutions may address better than others, for example, disability support or crèche facilities? Are you free to live and study in any location or do your commitments restrict you to a certain geographical area? Are you a mature student, overseas student, parent with dependent children or part-time student who would like to study in an environment with significant numbers of people in similar situations to yours? If these needs are met, you will feel more comfortable about integrating into your new environment and surroundings, so it is worth spending time researching what is available.

Do not dismiss any of your preferences as insignificant. Whilst specific obstacles can usually be overcome and, for example, you should not rule out the university that is the furthest from your home if it appeals to you the most, it is nevertheless sensible to weigh up the practical considerations if you are trying to narrow down a list of potential institutions in which you have equal interest. Don't expect this to be a straightforward process as each will have advantages and disadvantages in terms of your own personal criteria. You may find it helpful to write a list of the pros and cons of each before weighing them up against each other and making your final choice. You may also find that your preconceived views change completely when you attend an open day or interview. (See also the relevant checklist in Chapter 11 – *Have you decided on your shortlist of institutions?*)

▶ Student concerns

Most students are both excited and concerned about going to university. The freedom that is associated with independent living is seen as a key benefit and many students look forward to answering only to themselves, organising their own work and social timetable, and focusing on their own preferences. However, many are simultaneously apprehensive about certain aspects of student life – in particular, managing finances, coping with domestic life, dealing with university study, establishing new friendships and becoming part of the social scene. Nearly all students approach university life with a set of expectations, and these are most likely to be realised if the individual concerned has spent time identifying his or her preferences and trying to effect a good match when choosing where to go to university. Students are also less likely to be disappointed if they are prepared to be patient and not expect everything to fall into place instantly. Whilst it is not possible to know in advance the extent to which one will fit in and thrive within a new environment, knowing what you want and researching which institutions are most likely to offer it can go a long way in ensuring that personal expectations are met. Similarly, a basic understanding of new skills required in student life, such as the ability to budget and look after nutrition and domestic needs, help in ensuring a smooth transition to independent living. Subsequent chapters in this book will address specific areas in more detail, enabling students to identify what they need and want and ensuring that they are in possession of the necessary knowledge and skills to deal with the situations outlined. Forewarned is forearmed, and time spent on research will guard against unwanted surprises and disappointments.

> *My expectations of university were very different to what I had envisaged mainly because American teen sitcoms played a large influential role.*
>
> (**Aled**, 1st-year undergraduate)

Once you embark upon student life, you will be responsible for making key decisions and choices. It therefore makes sense to give the important decision about where to go and how to organise your life when you get there due weight. Time spent evaluating all the options and identifying the optimum course of action will reap dividends in ensuring that your expectations are met.

▶ Summary

All universities are different, and students' choices are not based solely on academic considerations. Expectations of student life are also very important and individual requirements need to be acknowledged. This chapter has highlighted the key criteria to be taken into account when coming to a decision in order to help students identify their personal preferences and to equip them for making appropriate choices that best match their needs and aspirations.

▶ More Feedback . . .

❛ *When choosing a university, it was very important that I could find the right course as I am very specific in the areas of geography that I want to study. However, the impression that I got on open days was also important in my decisions. I had to be able to envisage myself in that university and city as I don't want to arrive somewhere and find it doesn't suit me. Apart from the course, I also wanted to know about the quality and cost of accommodation which is quite varied, and also the nightlife for weekend socialising* ❜

(**Sean**, sixth-former)

❛ *I think I'm quite well prepared for university – at home I do all my family's laundry anyway so that won't be a problem, and while I'm no Delia Smith, my culinary skills are fairly good. . . . Personally, I think that the option to do a year's work placement as part of my course is vital to ensure that I have as few problems as possible finding employment in the future. . . . I'm only considering universities which offer en-suite rooms in halls, as sharing a bathroom with five or six other students is a really grim thought!* ❜

(**Charlotte**, sixth-former)

❛ *When I chose xxx, I chose it because it was the second-best place in the country to study my subject, and most importantly it looked beautiful! I now realise that this was so stupid because it would have been a much better idea to choose a university because of what it offered in terms of a nightlife and life outside of uni. Then I would be enjoying uni a lot more. xxx is too small for me. I should have thought about this when choosing my uni. I did a gap year in which I spent a season snowboarding. It was the best time of my life, there was so much new to experience. When I came to uni I was so disappointed as I felt that I had gone back a step. Everyone was dealing with leaving home while I was waiting for the fun to start. It never did. I had always heard that university is meant to be the best time of my life. I now realise it is about working still!* ❜

(**Lesley**, 2nd-year undergraduate)

❛ *In terms of choosing a university what mattered to me at the time was staying close to home to be near my boyfriend (daft criteria but true . . . we split up after my second term!). Luckily I realised that it was more important to get into the best one that I could, that I did a course that I liked the sound of. I'm really glad I moved away because however daunting it may seem, living in at university is one of the best experiences there is.* ❜

(**Annabel**, 3rd-year undergraduate)

3 Leaving Home

This chapter will:

- consider the implications of leaving home
- identify how to prepare for independent living
- provide a checklist of what to take to university
- offer some insight into parental concerns

▶ Leaving home

For many students, attending university will mean leaving home for the first time. By this stage, most will be ready to take over the responsibility for their lives and will see this as one of the most positive and exciting aspects of going to university, as indeed it is. However, it may also seem a daunting prospect. Living at home usually entails abiding by a set of well-established rules and practices determined by others, whereas at university the individual concerned has the freedom to make personal lifestyle decisions with far fewer restrictions. However, at home it is likely that others shoulder most of the financial and domestic responsibilities, whereas at university the individual is solely responsible for managing her or his own situation. Moreover, this is not a gentle transition: one minute the student is living at home, and the next (s)he is living away. This can come somewhat as a shock to both students and parents and can mean that for students who have, to date, been content for their parents to do everything for them, there is little time to acquire and practise lifestyle skills. For these students the learning curve will be steeper but there is no reason why the outcome should not be successful.

> ❛ Leaving home will be a mixed experience. Obviously, to lose the support and warmth of family for half the year will be hard. But to gain my true independence; to be able to do what I want when I want will be very liberating. ❜
>
> (**Roddy**, sixth-former)

Going to university inevitably opens a doorway to many new experiences, and, similarly, leaving home leads to multiple new experiences too. This means that students who leave home to attend university simultaneously need to deal with two major changes in their lives. This chapter looks at some of the practical issues that these students need to consider in order to ease the transition. However, students who remain in the family home throughout their university years may also usefully benefit from reflecting on their new lifestyle and its implications. Now is a good time to redefine home rules to take into account the fact that university life calls for students to organise their own study, leisure and social schedules. It may be appropriate to negotiate for greater independent living, more freedom and less accountability.

> I think my mum will be a little bit lonely when I leave home for university because we are very close, but she has known that it will be happening for a long time and we have talked about it a lot. ... She has already planned to get a dog to keep her company.
>
> (**Sue**, sixth-former)

Although the combination of the major changes on the horizon may seem overwhelming to those who are leaving home for the first time, the majority of new undergraduates are in this position at the start of each new academic year and most are fairly swiftly able to establish routines and practices that work for them. There is plenty of help on hand at each university, and students can also make the transition easier by thinking through the implications of leaving home in advance and by making the necessary arrangements and plans before departing for university. Basically, there are two key components to starting undergraduate life on the right footing: identifying the skills required for independent living and going some way to acquiring them in advance, and making certain that you take what you need to university to ensure that day-to-day living is as smooth as possible. If you are on top of your lifestyle arrangements you will be able to focus all your energies on your studies and your new environment while managing your lifestyle calmly, and perhaps even subconsciously. If you are able to take care of yourself without becoming stressed about it, you will soon enjoy being in control of your life and thrive on the responsibility. Indeed, the sooner you are able to relax into your new lifestyle the better, as this will give you a strong framework within which you can explore all the advantages and freedoms that accompany life as an undergraduate. This chapter will therefore look at how you can prepare for independent living, before supplying a comprehensive account of what you might like to take with you to university.

Moving all my stuff here was a bit hard and having my family so far away has hit me harder than I thought it would.

(**Sophie**, 1st-year undergraduate)

▶ Preparing for independent living

When you go to university, in addition to managing your studies, you will need to be in control of your living arrangements. This will include shopping and cooking for yourself, ensuring that your room is clean, dealing with all necessary administration and making sure that you keep track of all relevant documentation, managing your finances, laundering your clothes and bed linen, and dealing with unexpected problems such as illness. These are all practical skills that must be acquired, and the key to success is to be sufficiently familiar and confident about them so as not to let them become stressful and too time-consuming. With this in mind, it is worth doing what you can before you leave to ensure that this is the case. Most potential problems can be avoided by making sure that you have what you need with you at university, not only in terms of useful items, but also in terms of skills. If you identify and address gaps in your life skills before you go, you will be able to cope with independent living. Forward planning can be very helpful here. (See also the relevant checklist in Chapter 11 – *What to do before going to university*.)

 Try not to take too many memories of home – too much can make you upset.

(**Claire**, 3rd-year undergraduate)

Administration and filing

Before you leave, set up a file in which you can keep all the important documents that relate to your new independent life, and start to organise it. Make sure that you use file dividers to denote separate areas as this file will get progressively more full during the term. Documents might include all correspondence with your landlord or accommodation officer, any relevant receipts, instructions for electrical goods, your licence if you have a TV, insurance documents and so on. You may wish to include correspondence you have had with the university in this file, particularly maps of the campus and details of societies you may wish to join. It is a good idea to put all useful paperwork in one place where you will easily be able to find it, as this will also ensure that you are able to deal with any problems quickly. If you can establish a filing system before you go, life will be simpler when you arrive, so get into the habit of filing relevant paperwork once you have read it. Students living at home will also benefit from a good filing system, and it is worth thinking about whether you need to reorganise your study bedroom at home to accommodate your new needs.

> *What not to take – your boyfriend/girlfriend on your first day! Old PJs – get a new pair.*
> (**Amber**, 3rd-year undergraduate)

Financial matters

You will also need a file devoted to your finances. It is very important that you keep on top of your income and expenditure and for this reason all details should be kept in one place. You may wish to request bank statements more frequently now that your finances are about to become more complicated. It is not necessary to change your branch unless you wish to, but you should advise your current branch of your new address so that you receive bank statements promptly. If you do not yet have a bank account, or you are considering changing banks, try to do your research before you go to university, so that your arrangements are in order when you go. If you are unclear about where you wish to hold an account, or about any aspects of managing it, collect all the relevant leaflets from the banks in good time and, if necessary, make an appointment to talk to the personal banker or student adviser at the bank of your choice. You may also find useful information on your university's website. Think in advance about how you intend to keep track of your finances and whether you would prefer to use cash, cheques or credit cards. You may wish to apply for a debit card if you don't already have one, or to set up any direct debits in good time. (These choices will be explored further in Chapter 5.) If you are intending to undertake paid work whilst at university, include the relevant documentation in the file, such as your national insurance and tax details, and keep it up to date.

> *Remember – a bottle of wine or cans of beer will prove popular with your new friends. I did and thoroughly enjoyed my first night.*
> (**Jasmine**, 3rd-year undergraduate)

Shopping

If you have never shopped for yourself it would be wise to look round a supermarket and get an idea of the products on offer together with a general overview of what things cost. It is sometimes surprising to note what is inexpensive and what is expensive, particularly in terms of food, and a general overall idea will help you to budget. You will also be able to see which items may be purchased in small quantities.

Cleaning

Cleaning is not difficult but it is not always immediately apparent which product is best for which job, or the type of cloth that should be used. Ensure that you find this out before going to university so that you could, if necessary, clean your room, the kitchen and the bathroom. Check out the products you have at home and how to use them.

Laundry

Ensure that you know at which temperature your various items of clothing and bed linen can be laundered. Domestic machines usually have a large range of programmes whereas machines in laundrettes may have only two or three settings. Check that you understand the manufacturers' instructions for what you intend to take with you, and also that you can recognise signs depicting, for example, when tumble drying is inappropriate. It is usually best to wash dark items together and whites separately, and if you spend time initially checking the requirements of what you intend to take, you will be able to leave out items with complicated instructions that may prove too time-consuming to launder. It is also a good idea to learn how to hand wash individual items such as jumpers, and to locate and operate the 'spin only' cycle on a machine. Have a trial run at home as this will give you the opportunity to spot any gaps in your knowledge, for example how much powder to use. As a rule of thumb, it is best to wash clothes at 40 degrees unless the labels state that washing at a higher temperature is appropriate.

If you have never ironed anything, now is the time to learn! It's a slow process at first but one at which proficiency can easily be achieved. Rather than guessing how to do it, watch an expert, and with practice it will soon become automatic. Check that you are clear as to how hot the iron should be for your clothes (denoted by dots on the washing label which increase in number from one to three according to how hot the iron should be), and note any special requirements, such as t-shirts with transfers which need to be ironed inside out.

 Take your own plates and cooking utensils. Students never clean! And take a TV and stereo.

(**Conor**, 3rd-year undergraduate)

Cooking

If you have never cooked, start paying attention when those around you are cooking; take heed of recipes that would be easy to reproduce and write them down in your own notebook. Practise one or two easy dishes or snacks before you go to university so that you have a basic repertoire. You do not have to be an expert cook to follow a nutritious and balanced diet. Make a mental note of food that can be eaten raw or with the minimum of prepara-tion. Tie this in with your observations about the cost of various items in the supermarket, so that you go to university with ideas about how you will feed yourself. Do not feel embarrassed to ask your family for advice and help. They will feel happier in the knowledge that you will be eating properly and you may find that producing your own simple meals at university is more enjoyable and healthy than the alternatives. (See also Chapter 8.)

Maintenance
If you are going to be renting a room in a shared flat or house in the private sector, it might be wise to ensure that you have some very basic mainte-nance skills, as even if it is your landlord's responsibility, you may find it quicker and easier to deal with small problems yourself. Have a look in your current home where to turn off the water and electricity so that this is not a mystery to you in your new flat. Make sure that you know how to change a fuse, rewire a plug and unblock a sink.

Students living at home throughout their university years may find that they are not expected to clean, cook or do their own laundry. However, nice though it is to have others do these tasks for you, you may wish to become more self-sufficient and independent at this point.

▶ What to take to university

In addition to acquiring some basic knowledge and skills, as outlined above, it is important to think carefully about what you would like to take with you when you leave home. There is no definitive list of what students should take to university because it depends on the type of accommodation involved, the means of transport from home to university and the individual's personal preferences. Some people are happy with a minimum of personal effects in their new environment whilst others are more comfortable surrounded by their own possessions. It is advisable to compile a full list of all you might like to have with you, but only to take the bare essentials at first. That way, it will be a simple matter to amend your list once you have had a chance to evaluate what is provided, and collect anything else you may need at a later date. Also, you will be able to establish whether or not there is a facility for storing any of your possessions at university during the vacations and this may affect how much you take. If storage is available, you may choose to transport your belongings in stackable plastic crates with lids, as these are more robust than cardboard boxes and offer better protection for their contents whilst in storage. After your initial journey you will also have a clearer idea of how much luggage you can feasibly fit into the car or take on the train, and it is better to underestimate rather than to overestimate initially. Take your time in making your list, and add to it as new thoughts occur to you. It is worth making your list well in advance as this will allow you time to ask family and friends if they have spare items that you can take. Also, some people may wish to buy you a gift to take with you, and your list will indicate what you would really appreciate. Similarly, if you have an imminent birthday, the list could be very useful.

> ❛ *I didn't realise it took so long to move all of my stuff from one place to the other.* ❜
>
> (**Andy**, 1st-year undergraduate)

You may find it helpful to categorise your requirements under different headings. These may include studying, finding and undertaking paid work, keeping your accommodation clean, cooking, ensuring that you have sufficient and appropriate clothing and any equipment required for hobbies, personalising your environment and dealing with the unexpected. (See also the relevant checklist in Chapter 11 – *What to take to university*.)

> ❛ *The first day I moved in to my halls of residence, I was excited but really nervous. . . . After hauling everything up two flights of stairs to my flat, I started to unpack. I decided to leave my door open so if anyone walked past they could say 'hi', so I didn't have to walk into a room of eight other people, which seemed rather daunting.* ❜
>
> (**Amelia**, 1st-year undergraduate)

Study

You will be able to acquire most of what you need after you arrive but it is still sensible to make your list in advance in case there are spares at home and you have the benefit of a car for your initial journey. Bookshops in the vicinity of the university are likely to have taken heed of reading lists and should offer a good range of texts, and you may be able to buy some books second-hand from previous first-year students when you arrive. Many universities have discounted stationery outlets which are cheaper than the high street equivalents. However, you may wish to take your key college or

A-level books if you are likely to be covering similar areas, or indeed, some of your notes. You may also find it useful to take basic reference books such as a dictionary. Although you will be able to use university computers and printers, many students find it worth the extra expense to have their own laptop and printer as this means that they can be more flexible about when and where they work. You may also prefer to take basic items of stationery with you so that you are immediately self-sufficient. Moreover, as well as the usual pens, ink, pencils, ruler, Tipp-Ex, paper and so on, you may wish to have your own hole punch, stapler, scissors and sticky tape. These items are often taken for granted when you live at home, but it can be very irritating to find that they are not at hand when you suddenly need them. Students living at home may also find that they need additional items of furniture in order to organise study materials, such as a book case or a filing cabinet.

Paid work

If you are likely to be working part time while you are at university, you need to take appropriate clothing. If you intend to look for work when you arrive, it may be a good idea to include a smart outfit for interviews. In terms of documentation, you should ensure that you know your national insurance number and have any relevant tax records. You will also need copies of your CV together with any references you may have from previous jobs, as these are testimony to your reliability and experience. If you do not have references it would be a good idea to organise and acquire these before you leave and to take several photocopies.

Clothing and personal effects

There is no dress code for university and you can wear what you like. However, when deciding what to take, you should bear in mind how frequently you intend to launder your clothes and how much ironing you are prepared to do. You may opt to avoid items that cannot be laundered in a washing machine, or cannot be tumble dried, or require careful ironing. As it is likely that you will have to walk some distance to attend lectures, seminars and so on, a waterproof coat and robust shoes would be very useful. Although coat hangers are often provided, there never seem to be enough. You may wish to take spares as it can be very irritating to run out when your unpacking is in full swing.

 It's always very daunting when you meet new people and I remember not wanting to come out of my room the first night!
(**Hannah**, 3rd-year undergraduate)

You will probably be required to supply your own bed linen, and for the reasons noted above, you may find 'easycare' items more convenient. A bottle of hand-washing solution may also be useful for laundering individual items, and if you are likely to have to deal with damp washing you may wish to purchase a clothes airer or a frame for small items that can be attached to a radiator. You will also need towels and a personal wash kit.

Many students like to personalise their rooms with posters but there are often rules about how these may be fixed to the walls. If you can find this out in advance it will mean that you can bring posters and Blu-Tack or drawing pins with you and decorate your room immediately, which will make it feel like home more quickly. You may also wish to bring an iPod, MP3 player, CD player or equivalent, television (for which you will need to buy a licence) or radio. Do not forget any special equipment or clothing that you may need for your hobbies, and finally, ensure that you have an alarm clock, not only to wake you up in the morning, but also to ensure that you do not miss key appointments in the early weeks when you may not automatically remember your timetable.

> *When I left for uni I wasn't expecting to miss home so much, but I did. Incredibly! I missed the cosiness of home life and the structure of family ways. What made it easier was making my room feel as familiar and lovely as possible – lots of plants, rugs, pictures, vases, junk etc.*
>
> (**Flora**, 3rd-year undergraduate)

Domestic requirements

Even if you are in a hall of residence with catering facilities and cleaning staff, you may nevertheless need to clean your room from time to time and supply some of your own meals. Whilst it is likely that you will be able to borrow large items such as a vacuum cleaner, you may find it useful to take a duster and cleaning cloth. If you are sharing a bathroom you may opt to take some basic cleaning products.

> *Whatever you take gives your new housemates an insight into YOU! I took a student cookbook and was informed that it would indeed make a good fire should it get cold at night. You can't go wrong if you bring beer. Drink it to celebrate or to commiserate. Everyone's a winner.*
>
> (**Paul**, 3rd-year undergraduate)

In terms of catering, even if crockery, cutlery and utensils are provided, you may find that for a variety of reasons you prefer to have your own basic supply. You may discover that your hall mates use the kitchen and do not clear away or wash up after themselves, or you may in any case wish to prepare simple snacks in your room. Basic requirements include a plate, mug, knife, fork, spoon, sharp knife, chopping board, saucepan, wooden spoon, colander, small oven-proof dish and a dish suitable for the microwave, together with any favourite recipes you may have. You may also prefer to keep your own tea towels and washing-up liquid. It is also useful to have a container suitable for storing food such as bread, cake or biscuits. Some students prefer to keep a small kettle and toaster in their rooms as this means that drinks and snacks are never a problem. You may also wish to have your own tin opener, bottle opener and corkscrew as it can be disastrous if communal items such as these go missing.

> [Remember] a toaster, kettle, tea bags, and definitely forget the sugar so you can make friends while asking to borrow sugar from the neighbours! Seriously though – pictures of your family and friends as they are always good to have around your room to make you feel at home.
>
> (**Ellie**, 3rd-year undergraduate)

> Remember to ask if you need a TV aerial lead as sometimes there is a socket in the wall and not a lead. And remember a marker pen to label your food.
>
> (**Anne**, 3rd-year undergraduate)

In terms of food, it is wise to ensure that you can feed yourself if you are in the middle of an essay crisis and don't have time to go out, or if you don't feel well. Essential items include tea bags, coffee, sugar, powdered milk (for those days when you have run out of fresh milk), something that you can put on toast such as jam or Marmite, and some tins or packets of soup. If you intend to make your own meals, you might also keep dried pasta, rice, cooking oil, stock cubes, salt and pepper, tomato purée, fruit, onions, a couple of large potatoes for baking, and a selection of useful tinned food including tuna, beans and tomatoes. If you have access to a fridge you could also keep butter and cheese. On a daily basis, it is always useful to have fresh milk and bread, and you may find it helpful to have some sort of a rota with other students for the supply of these items to avoid wastage.

Documents

You are likely to need several passport photographs in order to join various clubs and societies, borrow books from the library and so on. You will also need your NHS details when you register with your new GP (see Chapter 8), and since you may be asked to provide identification for a number of reasons, such as renting from a landlord, it would be useful to take your passport and driving licence. You should take all correspondence with the university in case you need to refer to it in the early weeks, and also your bank details, loan correspondence and any insurance documents.

Miscellaneous

Ensure that you are able to contact family and friends by taking an up-to-date address and telephone book, and either a mobile phone, phone card or change for a public telephone. You may also like to take some family photos.

 Bring multi-vitamins and plenty of clean underwear.
(**James**, 3rd-year undergraduate)

Before you complete your list, try to think of items that you probably take for granted at home but that are difficult to do without in an emergency. In addition to any personal medication, you may wish to stock up on a few basics such as cold remedies, headache tablets and so on. A screwdriver and a couple of spare fuses are also likely to come in handy, as is a basic sewing kit comprising pins, needles and cotton, so that you can deal with any small repairs to your clothes such as loose buttons. And some students keep a spare toilet roll in their room in case the communal supplies are not replenished sufficiently frequently!

 Take sensible going-out shoes as a lot of time is spent out and about getting to know people. Also, a sense of humour – no one likes someone that complains a lot.
(**Daniel**, 3rd-year undergraduate)

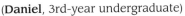

▶ Parental concerns

Do not be surprised if your parents appear to be increasingly concerned as the time for your departure to university approaches. Although you are likely to have made your own key decisions for some time, and to have lived with a measure of independence, your imminent move is a stark and sudden reminder that you are an adult and that from now on you will be looking after yourself in every respect on a day-to-day basis. Most parents will instinctively ask themselves whether they have sufficiently prepared you for this and many will have concerns, particularly those who have ensured that your clothes are washed, your room is cleaned, your meals are put in front of you and the parental taxi is at your disposal.

> *Keep hold of leaflets from freshers' fair. They give lots of money-off vouchers for clubs and bars and also tell you what's on when.*
> (**Ruby**, 3rd-year undergraduate)

Most worries will centre on parents' perception of your ability for independent living and making your own decisions. Until now they have been able to monitor you and ensure that you are not devoting what they consider to be too much or too little time and attention on various aspects of your life. Once you have gone to university you will be monitoring yourself, making plans accordingly, and imposing self-discipline when necessary. It is perhaps unsurprising that such a sudden development provokes a strong reaction as parental doubts come to the fore. Your best course of action is to listen to any concerns raised and to use them as your own personal checklist for assessing whether you do have the skills necessary to cope. If you honestly feel that they have a point, there is ample time to remedy the situation before you leave. This may involve discussing the issue concerned, honing your domestic skills or acquiring items that will alleviate the situation. This may also work to your advantage in material terms as in some cases parents may be willing to pay for what it takes to ensure their own peace of mind, for example a mobile phone to encourage you to keep in touch. Take advantage of your parents' concerns and ask them to help you acquire any domestic skills that you feel may be lacking, such as the ability to cook simple meals or launder clothes – it makes sense to benefit from their experience and knowledge of you, and to use their comments to ensure that by the time you leave you are well equipped for independent living.

> *Teabags are an essential tool in bridging the gap between you and your new flatmates. There is nothing a sit down and a cup of tea cannot resolve. Don't forget the milk and sugar. I also feel a good standard chocolate digestive goes down well.*
> (**Danny**, 3rd-year undergraduate)

▶ **Summary**

This chapter has focused on what it means to leave home. It has identified the specific domestic skills that are required for independent living and suggested how students can ensure that they are well prepared by the time they go to university. It has also examined what students should take with them in order to make their lifestyle away from home more comfortable and problem free. Finally, it has offered some insight into parental concerns.

▶ **More Feedback**

> By the time the summer came around I was bored rigid with living with my parents. So I was looking forward to the freedom of choosing my own things to eat, watching the TV I wanted to, and generally having my own space. The weekend I left, however, was petrifying. I had an army of family and friends who seemed to do all the moving in so when I came to use my things I had no idea where they were being kept! Watching my parents, my sister, and my boyfriend walk down the corridor and out to the car, I just felt bewildered. It had all happened so fast. In fact, all of this first semester has gone pretty fast. I don't even remember the names of people I met in the first week. Trust me, it's so quick, it just flies by and there really is no time to be scared.
>
> (**Hilary**, 1st-year undergraduate)

> I think I'm prepared. I can cook a wide range of meals and can sort my laundry and stuff out. Difficulties could include too much drinking, especially in freshers' week.
>
> (**Alistair**, sixth-former)

> I found leaving home quite daunting at first as I'd never lived away from my family before. But on the first day I spoke to one of my flatmates about the trouble I was having setting up my TV, and he offered his help. We ended up having a laugh and he has become one of my best mates. On that first night I forced myself to talk to each of my flatmates and I realised I have a lot in common with them all. We now all go out together in the evenings, to the pub or the union.
>
> (**Caroline**, 1st-year undergraduate)

❛ *When my daughter went off to university I was full of pride and excitement for her, but also gripped by apprehension. One of the main areas for concern when one's child moves away is that the parental safety net is gone and they have to make judgements and decisions for themselves. As with all freshers, she overdid things in week one and for weeks two and three had freshers' flu. This was the time when she was very low before her immune system recovered and she got over the bout of extreme exhaustion and home-sickness. She has never been prescribed so many antibiotics in her whole life as she was in those years at uni! For the parents also this is a time for adjustment. On returning home from the delivery trip, at the first glimpse of her bedroom I dissolved into tears. The walls were bare and the surfaces saw the first light of day for many years. The very soul had gone. There were no special (sometimes unreasonable!) menu requests, no late nights worrying about what time the key would turn in the front door enabling the parents to finally drift off to sleep. The house was ours for the first time.* ❜

(**Lorraine**, parent)

❛ *It was a big shock to the system when I left all my family behind, realising that I was going to wake up and not be in the safety net of my parents' home. When I eventually got to my halls on moving-in day, and met all my flatmates, excitement took over. . . . It was strange how quickly we all felt comfortable with each other, which thinking about it was probably down to sharing a toilet and shower, and seeing each other half naked and vulnerably drunk in freshers' week. It was odd when freshers' week ended and the work started, because it still felt like a holiday, so getting into the working spirit wasn't that easy. We all found it hard getting up at 10.00 a.m., which sounds ridiculous, especially because I used to get up just weeks before at 7.30 a.m. I'm putting it down to the late nights and copious amounts of alcohol, but I wouldn't change it for the world. There have been times when I felt homesick and for a little while I felt like I was in limbo, questioning whether I should be here or not, but then not feeling like I could go home. But eight weeks on I feel truly settled and have met an amazing group of friends. So, no regrets!* ❜

(**Grace**, 1st-year undergraduate)

‘ On the day that I was taken to university by my parents and boyfriend I was an emotional wreck. When they left and I was alone in my room, I didn't want to leave it but I didn't particularly want to stay in it either. I realised that the only way to stop feeling like I was alone was to go and find some new friends. ’

(**Annabel**, 3rd-year undergraduate)

‘ Practically, leaving home was very difficult as I was moving overseas and I was unable to take so many things on the plane – things like plates, cups, toaster, hangers and a TV had to be bought over here in the couple of days my parents were here with me. I think I've gotten used to living alone quite quickly. I must admit my cooking isn't exactly wonderful, though who would have thought you could practically live on supernoodles and toast? Emotionally it was hard during the first week as I didn't know anyone and it's a whole different situation to be living in. You do adapt quite quickly. As I live abroad I am unable to visit home very often, unlike many people around me who went home every weekend, leaving the campus very quiet at weekends and then coming back on Monday talking about having been at home. This made me miss home very much. The one time I did go home during term time was fantastic as I saw my family and friends and instantly felt better. But when I did go back on Monday morning it was very difficult to leave again, more difficult than the first time, and I found myself in tears on the plane. My advice is to make the most of freshers' week if you have one, even if you don't drink you can still go out. Most of the friends I have made this year I met during freshers' week. Go out, have fun, relax and just be yourself! ’

(**Stephanie**, 1st-year undergraduate)

‘ I found that I did the most random activities, many that didn't interest me at all, e.g. going to a snooker club at 2 a.m. just so I'd fit in and make friends during freshers' week. Looking back, the freshers' week events are not the be all and end all of university social life. Pace yourself, you'll find who you like and dislike in due course. Three years is quite a long time. It's a marathon and not a sprint. ’

(**Mark**, 3rd-year undergraduate)

' *No matter how much you pack you will always, always forget a hole punch and toilet roll! You'll arrive with the car packed full. You'll be jammed in the back with a suitcase full of baked beans on one side of you and a mystery bag of 'essentials' on the other side of you. Always remember that the beautiful leafy pot plant you bought will definitely be dead within two weeks, and watering it with beer does not work. I don't know where I'd be without my toaster, a true life saver when you've only got 10 minutes to get to lectures. Other useful electrical goods are kettles (for copious amounts of black coffee), a sandwich toaster and an iron. I promise that piling books on top of clothing instead of ironing does not work!* '

(**Annette**, 3rd-year undergraduate)

' *I couldn't be without my music. In hindsight it's a lot more compact and easier to take your CD collection and copy them to your computer. It saves space and a cheap cable can enable you to have your computer play through your stereo. My TV and stereo and computer to me are all essentials.* '

(**Joseph**, 3rd-year undergraduate)

4 Socialising

This chapter will focus on university social life and what it's like to be a fresher. It will:

- outline what to expect in the first few days
- describe some typical freshers' events
- give an account of what the students' union can offer in terms of support and recreational activities
- offer examples of extracurricular pursuits
- look at wider opportunities, such as UK and overseas travel
- consider some of the problems experienced by new students, such as homesickness and loneliness

▶ The first few days

When you first arrive at university, you are likely to be struck by the apparent chaos that surrounds you. Hundreds of new undergraduates, many of whom are unfamiliar with their surroundings, will be milling around, making frequent trips to and from the car park with boxes and luggage, saying goodbye to parents and family, and generally trying to get organised. Then, after a flurry of activity, the families depart, and the new students are left to unpack their belongings and prepare for the term ahead. At this point the atmosphere can become strangely quiet: people don't yet know each other so many opt to remain alone in their rooms. It can seem like an anti-climax after a big build-up, but don't worry; this is only a temporary lull!

❛ *Everyone will be in the same boat, but the idea of being alone, albeit only for a while, is a worrying one.* ❜

(**Elizabeth**, sixth-former)

As lectures will not begin for a few days, this is your opportunity to get to know your neighbours and your new location, and to complete a few administrative tasks. (See also the relevant checklist in Chapter 11 – *What to do in the first few days at university*). You will meet a great number of new people in the first few days at university, and you may wish to jot their names down when you get back to your room so that you don't forget who is who. However, all the clichés you may have read about freshers' week are true: it's common for students to team up initially with people with whom they rarely spend time after the first few weeks, and everyone seems to ask the same questions about where you live, your A-levels and your course. Be prepared to repeat your stock answers endlessly with a smile as the settling-in process does actually work and eventually you will find your niche and establish your own group of friends. Events are arranged for freshers in the first week or so, providing plenty of opportunities to get to know other students, and you will also meet new people as you make your way through the administrative formalities. Do not underestimate how long it may take to complete the registration procedures and how much time you will spend queuing. You can use the time wisely by coming to terms with the campus map, chatting to other people while you are waiting, and reading your Freshers' Handbook. This book is a valuable source of information as it lists all the clubs and societies that you can join, identifies key people in the students' union whom you can approach for help on a number of issues, and gives information on your new location including recommendations on what to do and where to go in your free time. Remember that the key purpose of freshers' week is to enable you to settle in and feel comfortable in your new environment, so take it at your own pace, keep 'having fun' high on your agenda and chill out when you need to. Students who are living at home may find that with fewer formalities to deal with, they have a great deal of free time on their hands. Rather than going home, it's worth staying on campus and trying to get to know other freshers, so that you do not feel disadvantaged, in a social sense, by your living arrangements.

> ❝ *Social life in university can be where you build many of the social skills you use later in life.* ❞
>
> (**Alex**, 3rd-year undergraduate)

For students moving into new accommodation, it is a good idea to unpack the file containing all your correspondence with the university early on, as you may need to refer to it regularly. You should also unpack or buy tea, coffee and milk, so that you can take a break when you want, and so that you are in a position to get to know your hall/flatmates over a cup of tea. It is also worth making the necessary effort in the first few days to get organised for the term ahead, as when lectures start you may be short of time. In the first week you need to try to accomplish the following tasks:

▶ organise your room so that you can live and work in it, and find what you need easily;
▶ register with your department (and your faculty if necessary);
▶ ensure that there are no problems with your student loan arrangements;
▶ acquire all the timetables and core books you need to get started, and make a note of the date by which you have to select which modules to take;
▶ get a library card and acquaint yourself with the library hours, layout and procedures;
▶ obtain your students' union card and information about what the union can offer you;
▶ register with a GP or the university health centre (see Chapter 8);
▶ make sure you have the stationery you require for your studies;
▶ establish where to go for lectures and seminars and generally start to get to know your new location.

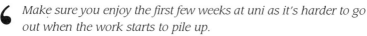

> *Make sure you enjoy the first few weeks at uni as it's harder to go out when the work starts to pile up.*
>
> (**Adam**, 3rd-year undergraduate)

▶ Freshers' events

Each students' union makes arrangements for the freshers, and although these vary from university to university, they generally include a Freshers' Ball and a Freshers' Fair. There may be many other events, and, if this is the case, it is sometimes possible to buy a 'season ticket' for all of them, which can represent good value for money. In addition to the events arranged by the union, your department or faculty is likely to organise at least one welcoming event. This normally takes the form of an introductory talk by a senior member of staff, followed by a chance to get to know fellow students over coffee or drinks. It is definitely worth attending functions of this nature, as it is important to find friends on your course. Not only will it be more pleasant attending lectures and seminars with people you know and like, but you will also be able to benefit from a division of labour when appropriate, such as by sharing out the reading requirements for a seminar and then discussing your findings if you do not have time to read all the books yourself (see Chapter 7).

> *Always be up for going out, going to events. Be friendly, make jokes, get drunk, have a laugh.*
> (**Charlie**, 3rd-year undergraduate)

Freshers' Ball

Although this sounds rather grand, the Fresher's Ball is generally an informal occasion involving an all-night disco and/or live band, together with a late bar extension. It is not normally restricted to freshers, and therefore offers the chance to meet students from other years. The balls are usually good fun, and often mark the end of freshers' week. If you are living at home, ask about the possibility of renting a guest room in a hall of residence for the night of the freshers' ball. This is obviously an added expense, but it will mean that you can enjoy the event without having to worry about getting home. Alternatively, you may find someone on your course who will let you stay with them for one night, or you may wish to organise a late taxi home.

> *Hopefully making friends will be easy, because there will be so many to choose from, and many will have similar interests to me. However, I do not drink, and I think drinking is a big part of student life, so I am a bit worried I won't fit in in that area.*
> (**Bernadette**, sixth-former)

> *Not everyone is into going out drinking and clubbing, me especially, so I set up the Sci-Fi, Fantasy and Horror Society. It is great for making friends and great for the CV. But don't forget that you will be living with the drinkers and clubbers, and 'preaching' to them about their lifestyle will not do you any favours.*
> (**Anne**, 3rd-year undergraduate)

Freshers' Fair

Another event not to be missed is the Freshers' Fair, the key purpose of which is to enable new undergraduates to see what is available in terms of clubs and societies, and also what local businesses, banks and so on have to offer. Many stalls offer free samples so it's worth viewing everything while you are there, and taking advantage of what is on offer. The clubs and societies use the fair to tout for business, but since joining involves a fee which is usually non-refundable, it is wise to think carefully about what you would like to do, and, realistically, how much free time you will have. Don't make too many spur-of-the-moment decisions at Freshers' Fair or you may find that you have spent a considerable amount of money on subscription fees to clubs that you are actually unlikely to attend. However, many societies offer a very cost-efficient opportunity to try new experiences, and it is a good idea to make the most of this. You can find a list of what is available in your Freshers' Handbook, and if you have the chance to read it and reflect on the contents prior to the fair, you will be less likely to sign up for activities on impulse. It may also be prudent to walk around the fair once, talking to representatives from all the societies you are considering joining, and then making a second tour with the purpose of signing up for your preferred choices.

> *The way that I have really fitted into university is by becoming involved with societies, and the social side of the students' union. I have met my friends through productions I did with theatre societies, and enjoyed spending time with these people through rehearsals and socially. It has been an exciting way of getting involved, really feeling like I fit into the small campus and have a place in it, and meeting plenty of new, like-minded people. It keeps you busy too, so that you never ever get bored, and makes going out socialising more of a reward. Sometimes I had to remind myself I was doing a course too!*
>
> *(**Francesca**, 3rd-year undergraduate)*

▶ Students' Union

Your local students' union is at the heart of the social life of the university, and you can obtain a union card once you have registered on your course. Almost all unions are also affiliated to the NUS (National Union of Students), enabling their members to enjoy the range of benefits that accompany the NUS card. The NUS's comprehensive website, www.nusonline.co.uk, contains useful advice and information on a wide range of issues affecting students, and has a special section for freshers. It also has separate sites for students in Scotland and Wales, which may be accessed via the main site. The appropriate website for students in Northern Ireland is www.nistudents.org.

The union offers advice, support and representation to members, although the nature of this varies according to the size of the institution. Some larger universities may have advice centres run by full-time staff; smaller ones may have a team of volunteers who give out literature on a variety of topics together with telephone numbers and addresses relevant to a range of problems. Some unions also offer active help to ensure the safety of their members, for example, by providing free escort services home after late-night functions for students living on campus. The union may also be responsible for compiling and publishing the *Freshers' Handbook* and other literature of interest to students. The union offers representation to members wherever this is deemed necessary so, unsurprisingly, the scope for its involvement is very large and may range from academic issues such as problems with course structures to social issues such as equal opportunity policy.

Through its 'entertainments' section, the union also offers commercial services to members, such as cheap bars, shops and sometimes sporting facilities, and social events. These vary from place to place but nearly always include discos and concerts, often featuring well-known bands and artistes, and may also involve themed club nights, quizzes and theatrical performances. The primary aim is to benefit members rather than to make money, so any profit is ploughed back into the union.

The students' union also provides an infrastructure for a wide range of affiliated clubs and societies which cater for students interested in almost anything: sport, politics, music, media, religion and more (see below). If your interest is not currently covered and you wish to set up a new society, you should approach the union.

Union officers are democratically elected and follow an agreed constitution. There is normally a president and an executive committee comprising either paid full-time sabbatical officers or unpaid, part-time, non-sabbatical officers or a combination of these. The executive committee is responsible for staff within the union's employ and for regulating events and services. Elected student representatives also play an important part in the running of the union, and any student wishing to become more involved may consider putting his or her name forward as a candidate at the appropriate time.

NUS card

If your local union is affiliated to the National Union of Students, you will be able to enjoy the benefits of the NUS card. The NUS has negotiated discounts and special offers for its members from a number of organisations including HMV, First Travel, Tiny.com, Pizza Hut, the AA, 02, Burger King, Index, Alpha Blue, UGC Cinemas, Endsleigh Insurance, The Gadget Shop, Topshop, Topman and some Students' Union shops.[42] These are all detailed in the NUS Booklet, obtained from your students' union. You can also find out about more discounts on the NUS website: www.nusonline.co.uk/specialoffers. Once you have registered your card with nusonline, you can opt to receive e-mails of extra offers to members, enter online competitions, and receive a monthly NUS e-newsletter.

▶ Extra-curricular opportunities at university

Clubs and societies

One of the highlights of university life is the large number of extra-curricular opportunities available to students. These include a vast range of clubs and societies. For sporting enthusiasts there is likely to be a comprehensive array of team and individual sports for all levels. (If you wish to try out for a university team you should investigate this possibility early on as the trials generally take place in the first few weeks of term.) Musicians can expect the opportunity to sing or play their instruments in a range of classical and contemporary music societies, or to join a non-performance group that focuses on listening to and appreciating music. There are likely to be societies for enthusiasts of film, drama, politics, public speaking, religion, art, computing, electronics, and many more. Now is a good time to take up a new interest or two or pursue a long-standing hobby within a new environment, and since it is not unusual to be offered a choice of more than 50 clubs and societies, you should be able to find something that appeals to you. Students who are living at home may find this a particularly good way of becoming involved in university life.

> ❝ My social life is centred around a university sports team. Being involved in such a team provides the opportunity to meet like-minded individuals and get very drunk with them! The team has given me some of the closest friends I have made at uni, who unfortunately know me very closely, mainly through socialising with them and telling my deepest darkest secrets in moments of weakness when I was not in an alcohol-free state of mind! ❞
>
> (**Daisy**, 3rd-year undergraduate)

Many undergraduates opt to join voluntary community action groups which benefit the local community. Projects undertaken may include running youth initiatives or offering practical assistance to the elderly. If you want to mix with the wider community outside the university, this may be an option for you. This type of activity may also help later on when you apply for employment as it gives your CV an extra dimension.

If you want to become more actively involved in college-based initiatives you could consider becoming a union representative, or contributing to the university newspaper, magazine or radio, or helping with RAG week. This is a fundraising initiative which raises money for charity though a series of conventional and unconventional events such as discos, concerts or sponsored eccentric activities which often entail dressing up in bizarre costumes and undertaking strange tasks. Volunteers are required to help with planning, administration, managing the budget, marketing events, producing the magazine that traditionally accompanies RAG week and chairing some of the activities. Getting involved is a good way of using your skills and getting to know new people.

> ❛ *I have kept fit playing hockey three times a week. The hockey club like most sports clubs has a good social scene and opened up opportunities to meet new people.* ❜
>
> (**Chiara**, 3rd-year undergraduate)

Even if none of the clubs and societies on offer particularly appeal to you, it is worth joining one or two in any case as this will enable you to meet new people. You may enjoy the meetings more than you anticipate and joining a club will also give you some fixed appointments and commitments during the settling-in period. Whilst you can usually join societies at any time in the academic year, it is much easier to integrate if you start with the other freshers.

> ❛ *Always go to as many social events as possible and introduce yourself to anyone. They are in the same situation as you; they don't know anyone either! Try and mix with different groups every week as you will gain more friends.* ❜
>
> (**Andy**, 1st-year undergraduate)

▶ Travel opportunities

In view of the concessions available, and the long vacations, many students opt to take the opportunity to travel while they are at university, both in the UK and further afield. After a few weeks at university you may feel that you want a short break and a change of scenery, particularly as your new colleagues are likely to come from different parts of the country and it may be possible to stay with them if they go home for the weekend. A Young Persons' Railcard can represent a good investment as it offers a discount of about a third off most rail fares in Britain. It is available to people aged between 16 and 25 or mature full-time students and, apart from having to start your journey after 10.00 a.m. Monday to Friday if you do not want to incur extra costs, there are few restrictions. (See www.railcard.co.uk.) Similarly, you may wish to buy an NX2 card if you wish to travel by coach as this offers a discount of about 30 per cent on National Express coach journeys for people aged between 16 and 26 (see www.nationalexpress.com).

Although when you first arrive at university, overseas travel may not be at the top of your agenda, it is worth finding out about the possibilities for inexpensive travel abroad, as you may decide to plan ahead for the summer vacation. Some clubs and societies organise overseas trips at low cost, as do certain departments and faculties. Or you may wish to get together with a group of friends and plan your own trip.

Think twice about starting a relationship with someone you live with, because you will have to live with them a whole year, regardless of how the relationship goes.
(**Mel**, 1st-year undergraduate)

There are a number of discounted services for students which can cut the costs of travel considerably. The ISIC (International Student Identity Card) is internationally accepted and offers holders discounts on many flights, buses, trains and ferries in addition to entrance to a number of museums, cultural sites, entertainments, attractions, youth hostels, hotels, bars and restaurants. ISIC holders also have access to a discount communications package including voicemail, e-mail, SMS and phone, and to a 24-hour emergency helpline. The card costs £7 and you can find out where to get one and what paperwork you need to take with you when you make your application by contacting the International Student Travel Confederation (www.istc.org). Young people under the age of 26 can also apply for a selection of inter-rail passes, the cost of which varies according to the areas visited and the duration of the pass. More information is available from www.raileurope.co.uk. There are a great many organisations offering discounted travel for students, and you may like to surf the web to find the best deals, always ensuring, of course, that any company you choose is a member of ABTA. One of the most popular companies used by students is STA Travel (08701 600599 or www.statravel.co.uk). This has 65 branches in UK universities or high streets and 450 branches worldwide. In addition to cheap travel deals, the website also provides comprehensive information on travel-related issues such as health, insurance, accommodation abroad and so on.

If you plan to travel abroad it is very important that you think ahead and ascertain what is required in addition to your tickets. As well as having a valid passport, you should ensure that you have adequate insurance for the journey and that you are in possession of an E111 form which gives rights to some medical treatment for UK residents who are temporarily in other EEA (European Economic Area) countries. At the moment, the system is to take an application for an E111 form together with the form itself to a Post Office. These are then stamped and the form handed back to the applicant.

However, the system is changing and from June 2004 many European countries started to use a new card scheme. It is anticipated that the UK will introduce the cards by 2006. It is important to remember that the treatment offered as a result of the E111 may not always be adequate, so it is essential to have good insurance cover too. You can find out more details about the E111 and other health advice for travellers on the Department of Health's website, www.dh.gov.uk.

The Foreign and Commonwealth Office has a travel advice unit that supplies detailed information on many aspects of travel, including visa advice and the safety status of various countries. It enables you to check whether travel to the country concerned is recommended or not (www.fco.gov.uk or telephone 0870 606 0290). You should also check whether or not you need vaccinations for your visit (see www.dh.gov.uk or www.travelhealth.co.uk). It's a very good idea to read about the country you intend to visit and also to do some research about where you might stay prior to leaving. There are numerous travel guides available, including the Rough Guide series (www.roughguides.co.uk), and good starting places for accommodation include the International Youth Hostel Federation (www.yha.org.uk), which has 4000 hostels in more than 80 countries, or travel companies such as STA Travel (www.statravel.co.uk).

▶ Problems encountered in the early days

Feeling anxious, homesick or negative

Planning a trip abroad may be the last thing on your mind in the early days, when, far from reflecting on the many new opportunities before you, you may be wondering if you will ever feel settled. You may even be experiencing doubts about your decision to go to university in the first place. Most new undergraduates go through a 'negative' period, in which their thoughts may be dominated by feelings of loneliness, anxiety, homesickness, or a combination of these. It's important to believe that you are not the only one feeling like this, even if those around you appear to be happy and coping well. Try to hang on in there – these emotions are normal, and hopefully they will fade away as you integrate into your new life. However, do not feel that you need to hide what is in your mind as your feelings are nothing to be ashamed about. It will help if you can rationalise why you are feeling the way you do and also if you are able talk through your problems and your own assessment of them with someone else.

In the first few weeks you may feel uncomfortable with your new lifestyle. Whilst others may appear to you to have fitted in already, you may find it difficult to feel enthusiastic about any of the events on offer and, in the absence of alternatives, you may find yourself in situations you would not normally choose. This can affect your self-perception as you may regard your behaviour as weak. Moreover, in between functions you may have little to do, yet be unable to relax and unwind due to anxieties about your new environment.

> *Before I came to uni, I was quite reclusive. I found there was no room for it. Had I not opened up to the new people around me, I would have been very lonely, compounded by the homesickness everyone feels, I would have had a very miserable time. Remember we're all in the same boat. Be friendly!*
> (**Harry**, 3rd-year undergraduate)

Understanding your feelings

Your feelings of isolation may be compounded by homesickness, particularly if this is the first time you have lived away from home. It is unsurprising that, faced with so many new experiences, you may crave security and familiarity. Negative feelings are common and can be exacerbated by the following:

► sudden changes in lifestyle;
► anticlimax on experiencing university after having looked forward to it for so long;
► studying a long way from home and feeling that it is therefore impractical to return more than occasionally;
► becoming overwhelmed with the perceived workload;
► not particularly liking the people with whom you are living;
► not immediately finding new friends with whom you feel comfortable;
► assuming that others are coping better than you and do not share your feelings;
► living away from home and having to fend for yourself domestically for the first time, particularly if you don't feel confident about your abilities.

If you are feeling homesick, phone home and talk it through with your family and friends. However, try not to give up too quickly and rush home at the first available opportunity as this will not help in the long term. It will mean that you are not around at times when other freshers are making a big effort to initiate friendships and may mean that you miss important social events. Overall it is likely to delay your acclimatisation to your new environment. Instead, you might suggest that your friends from home visit you at university. This is particularly important if you are hoping to combine a long-distance relationship with life at university. It will be better for you if your partner visits you and becomes part of your life at uni, rather than if you constantly go home and try to live two lives simultaneously. If you do go home in the early weeks, consider taking one of your fellow freshers with you as this will give you the opportunity to get to know each other better. Try to adapt your lifestyle to prevent feelings of loneliness and isolation becoming all-consuming but, above all, give yourself time to adjust. This is not normally an instant process and it is not unusual for it to take several weeks. It is also worth noting that whilst most students feel homesick at the start of the new academic year, others may feel fine initially before succumbing later on.

> *There is no single isolated thing which I found difficult. It boils down to a culmination of several interlinked things including being in a different city, being thrown into halls (which can be quite intimidating), getting used to independence, adjusting to first-year sleeping/drinking patterns.*
> (**Richard**, 3rd-year undergraduate)

Some students live at home during their undergraduate years, and if you are in this situation it is equally important that you carve a niche for yourself in the university social life. Although you may have an established group of friends at home, you should try to attend as many freshers' events as possible and make new friends at the university. Try not to rush home at the end of lectures each day but deliberately set an evening or two aside every week so that you can spend time socialising with your new colleagues. Don't miss out on large social functions either, such as important concerts or events. It is likely that by the time these take place you will have made friends and will be able to stay with them if the prospect of your journey home would spoil your enjoyment of the evening, but if not, try to arrange overnight accommodation on these one-off occasions so that you can join in. Most halls of residence have one or two rooms available for visitors. These are not cheap, but you may feel that the social benefits justify the cost.

> *I was a bit judgemental of people at uni to start off with as I did not want to go out all the time and concentrated on my work more. This did not really help me fit in and eventually I found a good balance between studying and socialising. My first impressions of everyone I met in freshers' week changed dramatically over the 3 years and people who I despised have actually become my good friends!*
> (**Laura**, 3rd-year undergraduate)

Positive suggestions

It may seem strange to admit to feelings of loneliness in a university town populated by thousands of students, yet most freshers do feel lonely and isolated at first. Simply speaking to others will help, so try to be brave and take the initiative. If you walk into a room where you don't know anyone, introduce yourself to someone else, or, if you can't face doing that, stand with a group and join in with the conversation when you feel ready. This is easier at first meetings of clubs and societies, where time has normally been allocated for introductions, so make sure that you have joined one or two.

If you can convince yourself that this is a passing phase and try to fill the time constructively, you will begin to feel better. Ensure that you are ready for the start of lectures and seminars and spend some time organising your filing system and timetables. Go for walks around the campus and check out arrangements for doing your laundry, using the library and so on. Make a note of the nearest grocery shop, Post Office, bakery, bank and bookshop. Buy any necessary items of stationery now that you will need in the coming weeks and generally prepare for your forthcoming studies. Whilst students are not expected to work in the first few days, but rather to focus on settling in, you may find it calming to get some books out of the library and do a small amount of introductory background reading.

A good strategy is to accept all invitations unless you really can't face what is on offer. Whilst they may not necessarily appeal, they present an opportunity to meet new people and make new friends. Once you have others with whom to share your thoughts and discuss your new experiences, student life will be much more enjoyable. Learn the names of your flatmates or the people who live closest to you and try to get to know them better. If there is a communal area in your accommodation such as a kitchen, buy a newspaper, make yourself a cup of tea, and inhabit it. Others may have the same idea. This way you will be able to enjoy the solitude of your room in combination with the social benefits of a communal space. Moreover, you do not have to be close friends with someone to go to functions together, so try to take the initiative and attend freshers' events with people you already know slightly. It will be more fun and less of an ordeal as it will remove the anxiety that you may be left standing on your own with nobody to talk to.

Seeking help

Don't blame yourself for your feelings or see them as a weakness. Remember that you have left home for the first time; that you probably haven't had to make new friends for several years, and that you have gone from being a big fish in a small pond with established friends and routines, to a new independent life in which socially you have to start again from the beginning. If possible, share your thoughts with another fresher and listen to their perspectives. If you can't do this and you feel unable to cope, contact student support services and ask to talk to a counsellor. If you would rather retain your anonymity, you could talk to one of the volunteers at Nightline or the Samaritans. Nightline is a confidential helpline run for students by students. Its aim is to enable students to talk through their problems in a non-judgemental and anonymous situation, and it is available through the night. You can obtain your local Nightline number from your University Welfare Office or by checking the noticeboards in the students' union. The number may also be listed on the back of student ID cards and beer mats in affiliated institutions. Alternatively, if you log onto www.nightline.niss.ac.uk and look under 'local nightlines' you will find details of local websites which include some contact details. All branches operate a telephone service and some have e-mail or drop-in facilities. The Samaritans is a 24-hour confidential helpline, and may be reached by phoning 08457 90 90 90. Alternatively, you can find details of your local branch from the website, www.samaritans.org.uk. If you think your feelings are really unlikely to change and you genuinely regret choosing to go to university, you should speak to your personal tutor as soon as you can. It is possible that by talking about your specific problems he or she may be able to find solutions that alleviate the situation.

> *I found that I was quite unhappy in the first year and I know several other students who have had similar experiences. It's difficult moving to a new city. I think the general view of student life is that it's a laugh a minute, especially for freshers, but it can be very difficult before you have had time to build up a circle of friends who you can really trust. I was worried about why I felt so awful and eventually went to the doctor. I'm so glad that I did because just talking it over with someone who took me seriously was so reassuring. In the second year I felt much happier, but if I had still been unhappy I would have gone to the Student Counselling Service. There is support available for students in that situation.*
>
> (**Henrietta**, 3rd-year undergraduate)

If you really believe that you have made the wrong decision, and you would like to leave, it is essential to talk things through with your personal tutor or another member of staff as they may be able to offer constructive advice that is specially relevant for your situation. It is particularly important that you seek guidance as you need to be aware of the implications on your future entitlement to student support should you wish to attend university at a later date. First-year students get a 'false start' which preserves many of their entitlements, but others who leave after the first year may lose one or more years of tuition fee and grant support. In addition, it is important to check the situation regarding your accommodation, as if you do not have a cancellation clause in your contract, you may be required to pay your rent/hall fees until the end of the term, semester or year, and you could be prosecuted if you fail to do this. Leaving university should be thought of as a last resort: if you talk your problems through with those qualified to help, solutions can usually be found. It is worth remembering that in most cases students do adjust to their new lifestyle and for many, their time at university ranks amongst the happiest periods of their lives.

It is very important that you do not let your negative feelings get out of control as this can result in a loss of self-esteem, which in turn makes attending social functions with new people even more difficult. Try to accept that settling in will take time and that it is not your fault that you feel the way you do. In the meantime, accept all invitations unless you really don't want to join in with what is suggested, and try to enjoy the time you do spend alone. Do not be afraid to plan solo outings if they appeal to you, for example a walk in the surrounding area or a trip to the cinema. Above all, respect your own ability to survive these difficult times, wait for them to improve, and do not be afraid to talk to others about how you feel.

▶ Summary

This chapter has focused on what it is like to be a fresher. It has given an indication of what the first few days at university are like and has described some of the typical events organised for freshers. It has drawn attention to the work of the students' union and the array of social and travel opportunities available to undergraduates, whilst giving advice on how to make the most of them. Settling in is not always easy and this chapter has also looked at some of the more common problems experienced by new students, such as loneliness, anxiety and homesickness.

▶ More Feedback . . .

 Having spoken to my partner, his friends and those around me who had already been to university, I had expected to have the time of my life when I started. However, for most of my first year I struggled to just even hold a conversation for two minutes.

Everyone seemed pleasant enough, but everyone wanted to be your best friend within the first five minutes of meeting you. This might seem quite nice for the first few days but after a while it did become quite tedious and lonely. I have lived on my own and fended for myself so that gap between home and uni life had already been crossed so I found it very difficult and very lonely. However, since then I have met a selection of people who are wonderful and who I can be myself with – it's been great.

(**Elisa**, 3rd-year undergraduate)

I have loved my time here and am getting quite depressed about it all coming to an end. One of the best things I did was to get a job at the students' union bar because you get to meet so many people. From that I got involved in clubs and societies and the executive committee, and I hope to run for office in January in order to prolong the university experience. What is great about xxxx is that it is a small campus so everyone knows each other – if you like a strong sense of community, it's awesome. To fit in socially, make sure you balance your social life and work – it's not all about getting a degree!

(**John**, 3rd-year undergraduate)

5 Finance

This chapter will look at student finance. It will:

- emphasise the need for devising and implementing a budget
- outline key areas of expenditure
- look at the policy regarding tuition fees
- provide information about student loans
- give an overview of the financial support available for students
- examine the options for borrowing money
- evaluate the advantages and disadvantages of part-time work
- give tips on how to save money
- supply useful contacts for further information

The importance of budgeting

Many students arrive at university with very little experience of managing a budget. This is generally because they have not been directly involved with the financial aspects of independent living: paying the bills, buying food, covering living expenses and so on. The result is that a great number of students do not have an accurate estimate of how much it costs to live as an undergraduate. Whilst being aware of the larger items such as tuition fees and accommodation costs, they may underestimate the amount that they will need to spend on food and daily life, and may also overlook some of the hidden costs such as photocopying fees, stationery, phone cards, insurance and so on. This basic lack of knowledge is compounded by the misguided assumption that the amount of income from loans, student support and so on, will automatically cover the costs. The figures for estimated annual income may seem large to someone who is inexperienced financially and has only previously dealt with small amounts of cash, but it is important not to be lulled into a false sense of security by this. Dividing the sum by the number of weeks over which it has to be stretched can immediately put it into a different perspective! The first step is to work out what money is required for the academic year and from where it may be obtained; the second is to devise an appropriate budget to ensure that essential outgoings can be covered; and the third is to stick to it!

> ❝ *I am quite confident in my ability to manage my money. However, large sums are involved so I do plan to seek advice from as many sources as possible.* ❞
>
> **(Elizabeth**, sixth-former)

▶ Estimating income and expenditure

It is a good idea to buy a notebook or file and devote it entirely to keeping track of your finances. If you do your accounts weekly or monthly, noting where the figures do not tally with your expectations and making the necessary adjustments, you will be more likely to make your budget work. In general terms, your income will come from a combination of the following sources: student loan; possible parental contribution; revenue from paid employment; grant, bursary or student financial support; bank overdraft and other credit facilities. Your outgoings will include some or all of the following: university tuition fees; accommodation; bills; food and living expenses; insurance; laundry; study costs such as books, stationery, photocopying fees; entertaining and travel (to and from the university; after late-night social events; to and from home); and miscellaneous items such as Christmas and birthday presents.

> ❝ *One of the best things I did in my first year was to keep a finance book. In it, I kept all my receipts, bills etc. so I knew what money I actually had! Putting a grand in your bank, at the beginning of every term is quite scary! Just keep a track of your money! As I finish my final year, I still keep a book but am much more relaxed about it all. I don't log every receipt like I used to. It has taught me money management! I'm still careful, but always know how much I can afford to spend. Keep some rainy day money for emergencies!* ❞
>
> **(Sharon**, 3rd-year undergraduate)

The best way to get to grips with budgeting is to understand your own situation thoroughly. A good starting point is to write a list of what you think everything will cost, preferably well in advance of your arrival at university. If you do not know what your accommodation costs are likely to be, you should ask the university accommodation office for guidance. Similarly, if you have friends at university, ask them what they spend on entertainment, food and so on. If you have no idea at all, you can look on the Internet for guidance. The NUS website, for example, contains a fact-sheet entitled *Managing Your Money*, which includes a breakdown of estimated living costs (see www.nusonline.co.uk). Similarly, the British Council's website (www.britishcouncil.org) also provides an estimate within its First Steps document, and although this is intended to help overseas students, the information is relevant to home students too. In the July 2004 press pack on Higher Education Student Finance, the NUS put the 2004/5 costs at £10,186 within London and £8584 outside London, to include tuition costs of £1125. The British Council estimated 2004/5 costs for nine months to be £7300 within London and £5936 outside London, excluding tuition costs. With these figures in mind, the combined potential income from loans, student support and other sources probably does not seem large after all.

Many students find it helpful to manage their finances by having two separate bank accounts. They use a current account for week-to-week living expenses, feeding funds into this from a higher interest rate account into which they place income from their student loan, student support, paid employment and so on. (Remember to fill in form R85 if you are a non-taxpayer so that any interest on your money will be paid free of tax. The form is available from your local tax office.) This system of two bank accounts prevents money 'vanishing' unexpectedly. However, in addition to this it is necessary to keep a basic record of income and expenditure so that you have a clear overview of what your lifestyle costs to maintain. If you keep records, this will also make it easier should you wish to discuss your financial situation with an adviser, for example, someone from your bank or the students' union. Whilst it might at first seem a chore, you will soon become more proficient at making notes and doing the necessary calculations. Moreover, it is a habit that will stand you in good stead in the future.

 I am concerned about my budget, expecially where it is supposed to come from and how I'm supposed to pay it back. No doubt I will become really tight!

(**Sue**, *sixth-former*)

Costs of studying at university

The main costs associated with studying at university are tuition fees and living expenses. As a result of government proposals in the Higher Education Act 2004, certain changes will come into effect in September 2006, and these will affect many areas of student finance. However, changes to funding in 2006 will only affect students who start in September 2006 or later, unless they have made arrangements to defer their entry for a year from 2005. If the student starts before 2006 (or is taking up a deferred place after that date), then for as long as they are on the course they will be funded under the old system.

> *I find the thought of being in debt for the next twenty years extremely depressing.*
>
> (**Bernadette**, sixth-former)

In view of the proposed changes, and since in any case there are differences between UK member countries, and also adjustments to the figures in question year on year, it is essential to keep abreast of the situation by checking the relevant websites. English and Welsh students should visit the DfES website, www.dfes.gov.uk; information is also available for Welsh students on the Welsh Assembly Government site www.learning.wales.gov.uk; students in Scotland should contact the Student Awards Agency for Scotland (SAAS), www.student-support-saas.gov.uk, and students living in Northern Ireland need to visit the Department for Employment and Learning (Northern Ireland) website on www.delni.gov.uk. The planned changes for 2006 (England and Wales) are also outlined in a DfES booklet, *The Future of Higher Education – a Brief Guide to the New Student Finance Arrangements.* Copies are available by telephoning 0800 731 9133. However, cross-border funding issues from 2006 (that is, what the Government will give a Scottish or Welsh student studying in England, or an English student studying in Scotland) have yet to be finalised.

The following sections cover arrangements in England. Separate sections later in this chapter focus on Wales, Scotland and Northern Ireland. The arrangements are broadly similar, although there are some key differences, which are noted.

> *Student life is very expensive for me. Travelling on the train every day for 25 minutes; trying to make up this extra money working in a video shop. Bored of being skint and not looking forward to paying off student loan. Hope it's all worth it.*
>
> (**Pat**, 1st-year undergraduate)

Tuition fees: situation for 2005/06 academic year in England

Full-time students starting higher education have had to contribute towards their tuition fees since 1998. For the 2005/6 academic year the maximum contribution was set at £1175. This figure represents about a quarter of the average cost of a course, and the balance is paid by the Government direct to the college. Many students attending designated courses have part or all of their tuition fees paid, and the amount of financial support available varies according to the individual's circumstances. For students who are dependent on parental support, their parents' residual income is taken into account, and for independent students, the family's residual income is assessed. Some part-time students are also eligible to have all or part of their fees paid (see Chapter 9). In 2005/6 full-time students from households with an income of less than £22,010 had all their fees paid by the Government, and students from households with an income of between £22,010 and £32,745 received some support. Under the old system, valid up until September 2006, tuition fees are paid up front.

Since the individual circumstances of each student vary considerably, it is essential to contact your LEA (local education authority), or equivalent if you live in Scotland or Northern Ireland, to find out whether or not you are entitled to support and how the regulations apply to you. If you do wish to claim support for tuition fees, the relevant form is available from your LEA or from www.studentfinance.co.uk. One single form covers applications for a student loan, fee support and many other categories of student support.

Tuition fees: situation after 2006 in England

From 2006, universities will be able to charge variable fees of up to £3000 for any full-time course. The variations will occur between courses within each university and not just between different universities. In order to charge more than the capped fee of around £1200, the universities concerned will have to sign an access agreement with the Office for Fair Access to show that they are actively involved in encouraging applications from sections of the community with traditionally low rates of participation in higher education. Moreover, OFFA will ensure that some of the extra money generated from variable tuition fees is assigned to bursaries for low-income students. Another key change is that fees will no longer have to be paid at the time of study. Eligible full-time students will be able to take out a student loan to cover the costs which will then be repaid after graduation when their future earnings reach a designated level (see below).

▶ Student loans

The majority of students starting higher education courses are eligible to take out a student loan to finance their living costs while they are at college or university. The amount of loan available depends on the specific financial circumstances of the individual concerned; where they live and study; which year of their course they are currently attending and the number of weeks in their academic year. The loan is repaid after graduation when the individual's income reaches a specific level.

There are many sources of information about student support and student loans. Students in Scotland should contact the Student Awards Agency for Scotland (SAAS), www.student-support-saas.gov.uk, and students living in Northern Ireland need to visit the Department for Employment and Learning (Northern Ireland) website on www.delni.gov.uk. Key web resources for English and Welsh students include the Government's sites www.dfes.gov.uk, www.aimhigher.ac.uk and www.studentfinancedirect.co.uk. It is possible to download the relevant forms or apply online for a loan via the latter site. Various free guides containing detailed information about student finance are also available, for example, the DfES's publication, *Student Loans: A Guide to Terms and Conditions*. Copies may be ordered from the DfES information line, 0800 731 9133. The Student Loans Company (SLC) which acts on behalf of the relevant government departments in England and Wales, Scotland and Northern Ireland, in administering the student loans scheme, also has useful information on its website, www.slc.co.uk. Alternatively, you may find it helpful to discuss your queries with an adviser in the student support section at your LEA.

Arranging a loan – students in England

The procedure outlined below is generally common to all UK member countries, although there are some national variations, which will be noted in due course.

Applications for all types of student support, including a student loan, are made on one single form which may be obtained from your LEA or www.studentfinancedirect.co.uk. (This website can also provide contact details for your LEA should you need them.) In the 2005/6 session, the maximum loans available were as follows:

- ▶ £4195 – for students living away from home
- ▶ £5175 – for students living away from home in London
- ▶ £3320 – for students living at home[43]

(The figures for loans to cover the final year of study are less than those cited above, to reflect the fact that the graduate will be available for work from the summer onwards.) All eligible students may take out a loan for 75 per cent of the amount cited above, regardless of their income or financial situation, or that of their parents. The remaining 25 per cent is means tested. The LEA or equivalent is responsible for assessing applications for means-tested support. From September 2006 the maximum levels for loans will be raised to assist students in meeting their living costs, in this case for both new and existing students.

Since processing the forms takes time it is wise to apply well in advance, and notify the LEA and the SLC at a later date of any changes, for example if you opt later for an alternative course or institution. The forms are available from late January each year. Students who wish only to apply for non-income assessed support, that is, 75 per cent of the maximum student loan, are required to submit their application by 29 April, whilst those who wish to apply for means-tested support need to apply by 1 July. Once the paperwork has been processed by the relevant LEA or equivalent, the individual concerned is contacted by the SLC. A separate application is made for each academic year, and the forms are automatically sent to continuing students. You should expect to provide personal information in support of your application, together with evidence to verify your claim. Certain courses call for extra weeks of attendance, and in this instance the amount of the loan may be increased accordingly in view of the extra expenses incurred. Conversely, the rate of loan for final-year students is lower in that it does not take the summer vacation into account, assuming that individuals will be working or claiming benefits at this point.

If an application and details of your bank or building society account are received in good time, the loan will be paid in three instalments, at the beginning of each term. Students must notify the SLC and their LEA or equivalent of any changes in their circumstances so that the loan arrangements may be modified if necessary. The SLC sends yearly statements each autumn while the individual is in higher education, so keeping track of the situation is straightforward. If at any point you need further advice or assistance – for example, if you do not receive your payment – you can contact the SLC helpline on Freephone 0800 40 50 10, Monday to Friday, from 9.00 a.m. to 5.30 p.m.

Student loans represent cheap borrowing. They are subsidised by the Government, so students pay a much lower rate of interest than if they were to borrow from a commercial organisation such as a bank or a building society. The interest on a student loan is linked to the rate of inflation and limited to the bank base rate plus 1 per cent. Interest is charged from the day the loan starts and added to the final amount of the loan. These arrangements underpinning student loans mean that the individual does not repay more than he or she borrowed, in real terms.

Repaying the loan

Repayment does not begin until the April after you finish or leave your course, and only then if your income has reached a designated level. In 2004 this was set at £10,000 but the Government proposed that from 2005 individuals should not have to make repayments until their earnings rose above £15,000. These changes are in place now. Repayments are income-contingent; that is, they increase as income increases. An income of £16,000 would result in a monthly repayment of £7, representing 0.6 per cent of annual income, and a gross income of £20,000 per year would result in a monthly repayment of £37, representing 2.3 per cent of annual income.[44] Repayments are based on pay periods rather than annual earnings, meaning that variations in salary also mean variations in loan repayments. In most circumstances, the loan repayment is deducted at source through the PAYE scheme along with tax and National Insurance contributions, although for self-employed workers, loan repayments can be collected through self-assessment. Throughout the repayment period, the SLC sends out annual statements so that individuals can keep track of repayments.

The DfES booklet, *Student Loans: A Guide to Terms and Conditions*, which is available from the DfES information line 0800 731 9133, gives examples of repayment levels correlating to a range of earnings. It also provides further information for self-employed individuals and those with special circumstances. These include people living and working abroad, those with more than one job, those with more than one type of concurrent loan, and teachers on the RTL (Repayment of Teachers' Loans) Scheme.

Before any repayments are made, the SLC writes to outline how the funds will be collected. At that point you can opt to make extra repayments in order to clear your loan more quickly, if you so wish. Towards the end of the repayment period, the SLC may contact you again to enquire if you wish to repay the outstanding amount in a lump sum. Loans are cancelled under certain circumstances, for example if the individual becomes permanently disabled and unfit for work, reaches the age of 65, or dies. From 2006 loans remaining unpaid after 25 years will be written off by the Government, but only for new students.

▶ Other financial support for students

Although student loans must be repaid, many students qualify for financial support that is non-repayable. The nature and amount of student support varies from case to case so it is important to liaise with your LEA or equivalent to establish what is applicable to you. General information may be found in the DfES booklet *Financial Support for Higher Education Students*, which is available from the DfES information line, telephone number 0800 731 9133. The nature and extent of student support is constantly reappraised by the Government and from September 2006 non-repayable grants of up to £2700 per year for low-income students are planned, but for new students only. Continuing students remain in the old system. The information below is intended to give an indication of the type of support currently available. However, since it represents a general overview, it is advisable to seek further advice from both your LEA and your higher education institution about funding appropriate for specific circumstances.

Higher Education Grant

The Higher Education Grant was introduced in 2004. It is means tested, non-repayable, and intended to help with living and studying costs. In 2005 the maximum Higher Education grant available was £1000 and to qualify for the entire amount, students were required to have a household income of less than £15,580. However, students with a household income of less than £21,565 qualified for a proportion of the grant.

Specific groups of students

Funding is available to specific groups of students who may need support in order to study. These include students with children or adult dependants, disabled students or those studying part-time. (Specific support for the latter two groups is discussed in detail in Chapter 9, which also includes some relevant case studies.)

Students with children may qualify for support in a number of ways. These are outlined in the DfES booklet *Childcare Grant and Other Support for Student Parents in Higher Education*, available from the DfES information line. These include The Parents' Learning Allowance, designed to help students with dependent children with costs relating to their studies. This is means-tested and in 2005/6 the maximum amount available was £1365. Parents, whether or not they are students, with dependent children may also qualify for Child Tax Credit from the Inland Revenue. Further information about eligibility and the amount of support applicable to individual circumstances may be obtained from www.inlandrevenue.gov.uk/taxcredits or by telephoning 0800 500 222. Full-time students with dependent children in registered or approved childcare may also qualify for assistance with childcare costs. In 2005/6 the Childcare Grant for one child is £114.75 per week (85 per cent of actual costs of up to £135 per week), and £170 per week (85 per cent of actual costs of up to £200 per week) for two or more children. (These rates remain unchanged from the previous year.) Although full-time students do not usually have access to means-tested benefits such as housing benefit, students with children are often able to claim them, especially if they are lone parents. For further details see the NUS website www.officeronline. co.uk/library/infosheets.

Full-time students with adult dependants may be eligible for a means-tested Adult Dependants' Grant, which in 2004/5 was worth up to £2395.

Support may also be available for those studying specific courses. There are various teacher-training incentives, for example, and also National Health Service bursaries for health professional courses. Further details of teacher training support in England and Wales is available from the Teaching Information Line (0845 6000 991). The Department of Health booklet *Financial Health for Health Care Students* gives more information about NHS-funded support and is available from www.dh.gov.uk or telephone 08701 555 455. Degrees or diplomas in social work may attract funding from the General Social Care Council, and further information is available on their website: www.gscc.org.uk. The appropriate telephone number for information about NHS bursaries and support for health professional courses for students studying in England is 01253 655 655.

Further support once studying has started

UK students encountering financial difficulties once the course has started may apply for Access to Learning Funds through their college or university. The purpose of this is to cover costs not currently being met; to counter financial hardship; to help with emergency expenses; and to prevent students from giving up their course specifically as a result of funding difficulties. Certain students are considered to be a priority. These include those with children, mature students, low-income students, disabled students, those who have been in care or who are homeless, and final-year students. As with other support, the amount of assistance varies according to individual circumstances. Students wishing to find out more about the Access to Learning Funds should contact the student support office at their institution.

Certain students, for example medical and dental students, can claim back travelling expenses related to clinical placements after a certain amount (£280 in 2005/06). Further details are available from the NUS website www.officeronline.co.uk/library/infosheets.

Students in Wales

Whereas students in England will be liable to pay variable tuition fees from 2006, this is not the case in Wales. Students starting higher education courses in Wales, whether they are Welsh or English, will continue to pay the standard tuition fee (£1175 for 2005/06), although this will no longer need to be paid up front, as in the old system. From 2006 there will be loans available to assist with the cost of fees. From 2006 the Welsh Assembly will be responsible for student support for Welsh domiciles, whether they are studying in Wales or elsewhere in the UK. As yet, the picture for 2007 onwards is less clear as the Welsh Assembly Government has not announced a decision as to whether or not variable fees will be introduced or whether current students who have already started their courses will be exempt for the duration of their studies.

The financial support available to Welsh students is similar to that outlined above for English students. However, in addition, Welsh students may be entitled to the new Assembly Learning Grant which includes assistance for mature students and childcare. Further details may be obtained from www.learning.wales.gov.uk or www.dysgu.cymru.gov.uk. The Access to Learning Fund is also available in Wales, through the relevant college or university, although it is called the Financial Contingency Fund.

Details of teacher training support in Wales is available from the Teaching Information Line (0845 6000 991) or the Welsh Language Teaching Information Line (0845 6000 992), and the appropriate telephone number for information about NHS bursaries and support for health professional courses for those studying in Wales is 029 2026 1495. Funding for all these professions is different in each of the four nations.

Students in Scotland

Eligible Scottish domiciled students studying in Scotland have their fees met in full regardless of their financial situation or their household income. Scottish students studying in England are liable to pay the appropriate tuition fee for their course, and from 2006 the Scottish Executive will fund loans in order to enable Scottish students to deal with the issue of variable fees. In addition, depending on personal circumstances, some may be eligible for additional financial support. Eligible non-Scottish domiciled students from the UK who take a four- or five-year course in Scotland that is one year longer than the equivalent course in their home country, currently have the private contribution element of their final-year tuition fees met by the Scottish Executive. However, there are proposals to abolish this for new students starting in 2006 or later. The arrangement will be honoured for those who started in 2005 or before. There are plans to increase fees from 2006 for students from England, Northern Ireland and Wales who wish to study in Scotland, but at the time of writing the arrangements had not been finalised. Further details of all matters concerning student finance are available from the Student Awards Agency for Scotland (SAAS) website at www.saas.gov.uk.

At the end of their course, unless they meet the criteria for exemption, Scottish domiciled students and EU students who have studied in Scotland are liable to pay the Graduate Endowment if they receive a degree. For students who began courses in the 2004/5 session the amount of the endowment, payable in the April following graduation, was set at £2,154. This amount is increased by the rate of inflation for students who start in future years. The endowment is in recognition of the benefits graduates have received in the course of their higher education, and the funds that are collected from this source are put towards support for future students. Students may pay in a lump sum or take out a student loan to cover the endowment. Full details of liability, exemption criteria and payment arrangements are available from www.saas.gov.uk.

The overall amount of student loan available to Scottish students is the same as for English students. The maximum loan for first-year students is £3320 if they are living at home, £4195 if they are living away from home, or £5175 if they are living in London. Students who have to attend their course for more than 30 weeks of the year can apply for a higher loan. However, the proportion of the loan for Scottish students that is income-assessed is different than for English students, and varies according to whether the student is studying in Scotland or elsewhere in the UK.

Young (under 25 on the first day of the course), Scottish students who live and study in Scotland may be eligible for a means-tested, non-repayable Young Students' Bursary, to help meet their living costs. This is available for students from low-income families. Those from households with an annual income of £17,500 or less are entitled to the full bursary of £2395, and those from households with an income of up to £31,000 may receive a lower sum. An additional loan of up to £545 is available for those who are eligible for the Young Students' Bursary and whose household income is below £19,730.

Other financial support is currently available, such as the Young Students' Outside Scotland Bursary, which is for eligible students who started a course at a UK institution outside Scotland in 2002/3 or later; the Lone Parent Grant; Additional Childcare Grant for Lone Parents, and Care Leavers Grant. Travelling expenses may also be reimbursed in certain circumstances, whether or not the student lives at home or at university. These are means tested and are claimed on a separate form which is available on the SAAS website. There are also Hardship Funds and a Childcare Fund once the course has started, for those eligible. Further details are available from SAAS.

NHS bursaries and support for health professional courses are also available. The relevant telephone number for further information for students studying in Scotland is the SAAS helpline on 0845 111 1711. Funding for all these professions is different in each of the four nations.

Students in Northern Ireland

The current arrangements for students from Northern Ireland, in terms of tuition fees, bursaries and student support, are very similar to those for English students, outlined earlier in this chapter, with Support Funds being the equivalent of the Access to Learning Funds. As in England, from 2006 higher education providers in Norther Ireland are able to charge variable fees of up to £3000 per year for new full-time students. Existing students continue to pay fees of approximately £1200. Both new and current students may defer payment through a fee loan.

New full-time students from lower income households are eligible for a means-tested maintenance grant of up to £3200 and a maintenance loan. Existing students are eligible for the higher education bursary of up to £2000 per year.

Students from Northern Ireland studying at publicly funded universities or colleges in the Republic of Ireland have their tuition fees paid by the Irish Government. However, the institution in question makes a charge for registration, examination fees and student services, which in 2005 may be claimed back by the student concerned from his or her ELB (Education and Library Board). All student finance details, together with how to apply, may be found on the Department for Employment and Learning Northern Ireland's (DELNI) website, www.delni.gov.uk.

The appropriate telephone number for information about NHS bursaries and support for health professional courses for students studying in Northern Ireland is 02890 524 746. Funding for all these professions is different in each of the four nations.

▶ Borrowing money

It is relatively easy to borrow money. However, as different sources of borrowing involve different repayment terms, it is essential not only to know how much you need to borrow but, also, which are your best options.

If, like most students, your parents and family are unable to lend you money, your first port of call should be to the Student Loans Company. Student loans, as outlined above, do not attract the same rates of interest as commercial loans and therefore represent a cheaper form of borrowing. Moreover, you only need to start repaying the loan when you leave college or university.

Try to save as much as possible before you go to uni as it's really hard to get a job and hard to juggle one once you've got it.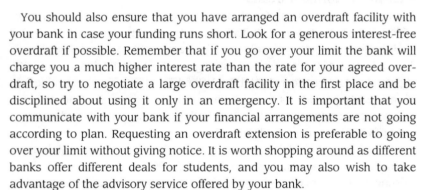
(**Conor**, 3rd-year undergraduate)

You should also ensure that you have arranged an overdraft facility with your bank in case your funding runs short. Look for a generous interest-free overdraft if possible. Remember that if you go over your limit the bank will charge you a much higher interest rate than the rate for your agreed overdraft, so try to negotiate a large overdraft facility in the first place and be disciplined about using it only in an emergency. It is important that you communicate with your bank if your financial arrangements are not going according to plan. Requesting an overdraft extension is preferable to going over your limit without giving notice. It is worth shopping around as different banks offer different deals for students, and you may also wish to take advantage of the advisory service offered by your bank.

Credit cards and store cards should be avoided whenever possible, as unless you repay the total amount each month, the interest will soon mount up. If you do opt for a credit card, check which one offers the best deal. You should look for the lowest APR (annual percentage rate) available as this will make a huge difference to your repayments. Credit cards tend to have APRs of up to 13–17 per cent whereas store cards can have APRs of up to 30 per cent. The Office of Fair Trading's leaflet, *Top Ten Credit Tips*, illustrates how much the repayments are on the different rates and can be downloaded from www.oft.gov.uk. Don't sign up for credit cards on the spur of the moment; don't be tempted by initial interest free periods, and seek advice from your union or bank manager if you are not clear about the conditions attached to any form of borrowing.

 Don't get a credit card!
(**James**, 3rd-year undergraduate)

If you do find that you are having difficulty making your repayments, you should talk to the people to whom you owe money and try to agree realistic repayments for the future, even if this means spreading them over a longer time. After that, prioritise your debts and cut out all non-essential spending. There are several confidential helplines and websites offering free counselling and advice on personal finance and debt. These include the Student Debtline (0800 328 1813) which is part of the Consumer Credit Counselling Service (CCCS) www.cccs.co.uk, Citizens Advice Bureau (www.adviceguide.

org.uk) and National Debtline (0808 808 4000 or www.nationaldebtline. co.uk).

Sponsorships and scholarships

Scholarships and sponsorships are another potential source of income, particularly for students who have a clear idea about their chosen career path. The Armed Services offer well-established sponsorship arrangements, as do some banks, accountancy firms, government departments and professional bodies. Sponsorship may include a salary or grant, or a financial contribution towards the costs associated with university study. It may also offer the opportunity for paid employment either in the vacation or during a sandwich period, and may also include free training.

You can get a basic overview of sponsorship and scholarship opportunities by referring to the various relevant directories that are likely to be in the Careers Office. These include current editions of the *Sponsorship and Funding Directory* and the *Educational Grants Directory*. You can also check out what is available by looking on the Internet. A good site is www.hothouses.com which offers a database of educational opportunities. Look under 'funding' and 'search for awards'. If you are specifically interested in sponsorship from a specific source, such as the Armed Forces, you can find comprehensive details on the relevant websites (www.army.mod.uk; www.royalnavy.mod. uk; www.raf.mod.uk). There are also subject-specific sites to explore, such as www.imeche.org.uk, the site for the Institution of Mechanical Engineers. Their magazine, *Engineering Opportunities*, can be downloaded free of charge at www.pepublishing.com/frm_magazines.htm and contains a directory with details of graduate sponsorship and sponsored university courses. Your Careers Officer will be able to recommend other sites appropriate to your individual course subject and interests.

The key advantage to sponsorship is that it often leads to a job with the sponsor after graduation. However, a disadvantage can be that it may only apply to certain subjects, and applicants may therefore be tempted to opt for a particular course primarily because the extra financial support is attractive. It is therefore important to consider the whole picture.

Many universities and professional institutions offer scholarships in particular subjects. However, competition is fierce and candidates generally need to attend additional interviews and possibly take extra examinations if they wish to be considered. Although the financial advantages may not necessarily be substantial, successful candidates do not normally have to fulfil work commitments as part of the arrangement, and furthermore, holding a scholarship may impress future employers.

► Paid employment

The majority of students take on paid employment during their undergraduate years. Indeed, for many, the income from paid employment is an essential contribution towards providing an adequate standard of living. However, although there may effectively be no choice but to take on paid work, it is important to think objectively about the nature of the work and, most particularly, the amount of time that can be given to earning as opposed to studying. Each student needs to consider his or her own individual circumstances and balance the need for income with the need to have sufficient time and space in which to study and learn. If undergraduate studies become too compressed, this may result in a lower degree classification at the final stage, and be counterproductive in the long term as it may limit career options and opportunities.

> *Get a job! Arrive a week early and find a job. Otherwise you will die from lack of a social life. Sponging off your parents doesn't qualify either.*
>
> **(Den**, 1st-year undergraduate)

If possible, it is better to work during the vacations rather than during the term. Many students live with their parents during vacations and do not have to worry about feeding themselves, visiting the laundrette and so on. Therefore they will not have to juggle work, studying and the pressures of independent living. Although there may be books to read, essays to write and projects to complete, the absence of lectures and seminars means that the days are largely uninterrupted, making it easier to take on full-time paid work for this limited period of time. If you had a part-time job before going to university, try to keep up your contacts, as it may be possible to return in the vacations.

> *By working a minimum of 12 hours a week, I can just about cope. This I find very difficult. I have had a job in a supermarket since my third week, and will only leave when my course ends. This has sometimes affected my work, but as my parents are unable to support me, I have no other choice. It also worries me that I will leave, although without an overdraft, in debt of £15,000 plus interest.*
>
> **(Sally**, 3rd-year undergraduate)

If you need to work during term time, you should think carefully about the advantages and disadvantages of different types of work. It is essential that you do not miss lectures, so try to establish your study commitments before taking employment. Your departmental secretary is a valuable source of information regarding the timetable, as even if it has not been finalised, he or she will have a good idea of how it has worked in the past, and when you are likely to be free. Some departments, for example, keep one day per week free of teaching commitments, and information such as this will help you to schedule your paid work at a time that fits in with your study arrangements. You also need to consider what you want to get out of working, over and above financial remuneration. If you know what you want to do after graduation and can possibly secure employment in that area, albeit at a junior level, this will stand you in good stead for the future as it will give you an insight into the sector and prove that you have a long-standing interest. If your career aspirations are somewhat vague, and, for example, you know that you want to work in finance but have not fine-tuned the details, try to find part-time work in a financial setting. This will not only provide you with relevant work experience but may help you define your future career direction. Check whether your course allows you to take a work placement module. If so, you may be able to use your part-time job as the basis for your written assignments.

 Have a job unless you have lots of money. About ten hours a week is enough time to study and go out.
(**Olivia**, 3rd-year undergraduate)

If you cannot link your part-time job to your future aspirations, think in terms of your individual skills and preferences. Do you have any qualifications that might enable you to secure a more specialised job that brings with it greater financial rewards? If you have your lifesaving certificate you could seek work at the local swimming pool/leisure centre. Similarly, if you have typing qualifications you may be able to sign on with a temp agency for single-day assignments. Have you worked in the past? Is your experience relevant to work you might find now? You might also consider the perks of certain jobs: babysitting may give you time to study once the children are asleep; gardening work may offer flexibility in terms of when the job is done; working in a bar will enable you to meet lots of new people, and working in the student union bar may be an excellent way of earning money without missing out on the student scene; working in a restaurant may mean regular, free meals. Give some thought as to what might work best for you.

Before you start at university, print out several copies of your CV and ensure that you have references. Contact the university job shop for advice on part-time work in the area and try to obtain a copy of the local newspaper. Register with any appropriate job agencies, and, if there are specific local employers for whom you would like to work, check their websites for possible opportunities, and send them a letter outlining what you are looking for. You may wish to check out www.morethanwork.net. This is a student employment advice site which has links to local job shops, created in collaboration with partners including the DfES, NUS, TUC, Uniservity, the NCWE and NASES.

Students who work are liable to pay tax and national insurance contributions if their income is above a specific level. The national insurance rules are complicated and vary according to whether the individual is an employee or is self-employed; tax is due on annual income exceeding £4895.[45] Further details on tax and national insurance payments, together with information on how to reclaim tax may be obtained on www.inlandrevenue.gov.uk. If you are a non-British student, there are several factors which influence whether or not you are entitled to take employment, the number of hours per week you may work and whether or not you need to pay tax and national insurance. Further details are available in UKCOSA's guidance notes, *Working during Your Studies*, available from www.ukcosa.org.uk, and from the Inland Revenue (website as above).

▶ Conserving your finances

Unfortunately it is a fact of life that most students have limited funds and leave university with considerable debts. However, there is a big difference between assuming that debt is inevitable and letting the situation get out of control, and living within your means and economising where possible. If you can possibly confine your debt to your student loan, repayment will not be so painful. Any money you borrow over and above your loan is likely to be costly in terms of interest repayments, so borrowing from other sources should be avoided if possible. There is a great deal of truth in the old adage, 'Take care of the pennies and the pounds will take care of themselves.'

 I find it a good plan to budget myself a certain amount each week, e.g. £40. Then I can plan how much to spend on food, socialising and treats!

(**Laura**, 3rd-year undergraduate)

The first step to achieving this is to devise a budget and stick to it, and the second is to look for money-saving offers and deals. When you plan your budget, be realistic about what you will need to spend on food and general living expenses, and allow yourself a certain amount of money for going out and entertainment, bearing in mind that you need to socialise but don't have unlimited funds. It is relatively easy to organise a budget but difficult to stick to it! Try to avoid impulse buys and items that you want but don't really need. Even if you genuinely do need the items, ask yourself if you can wait until the sales when they are likely to be cheaper, or if friends and relatives might consider contributing towards them for Christmas or your birthday. Don't be tempted to buy expensive items for your room or increase your wardrobe just because your loan has come through. Doing this might mean that later in the term you can't afford to go out at all or eat properly.

In terms of your weekly budget, it is important to adopt the attitude that you should not exceed what you have set aside for a particular purpose. For example, if you have spent your entertainment budget for the week, you should not spend any more money on going out until the following week. This may seem tough, but there are inexpensive alternatives, such as inviting friends to your room for coffee or to share a bottle of wine, joining friends in the union bar but sticking to one drink, or even setting aside an evening for some extra study! If you strive to keep to your budget, with practice you will become used to 'saving up' cash for going out, rather than wasting money simply because you didn't make alternative plans in good time. You will also become accomplished at eeking out your catering budget so that you are still able to eat healthily.

 Living on a small budget, which can often become a tiny budget, which sometimes is a non-existent budget, can get you down. But you get used to it and learn to enjoy all the innocent fun things to do with your friends again like simply spending time together, that you were content with as a child.

(**Hannah**, 3rd-year undergraduate)

It is also a good idea to take advantage of special deals and offers. Membership of the NUS brings with it discounts on a wide range of products (see www.nusonline.co.uk). Moreover, you have nothing to lose by asking for a student discount even if it is not advertised, so you should keep your student ID with you at all times in case you need it. Student societies are often cheap to join and can represent good value: for example, a film club showing a different film once a week is likely to be far less expensive than going to the cinema. It's also a good idea to investigate and take advantage of your university sports and social facilities. It is often possible to find cheap travel deals if you book in advance and, indeed, shopping around for most items can save you money (look at www.switchwithwhich.co.uk or www.moneysupermarket.com to find the best deals). Shopping with a friend can be cheaper as you will be able to take advantage of two-for-one super-market offers, or share newspaper purchases. Make sure that you sign up for a loyalty card for any of the supermarkets you will use frequently.

Keep a close eye on the student noticeboards. You may find advertise-ments for accommodation, offers to share petrol costs for specific journeys and many other good deals. You can also advertise on the boards if you are trying to purchase specific items, particularly second-hand books.

Hopefully, after graduation, you will swiftly be able to find employment and your financial situation will be easier. However, there will always be a need for budgeting, and your experiences as an undergraduate, together with the financial skills you have acquired during your life as a student, will stand you in good stead in the future.

▶ Summary

This chapter has highlighted the advantages of planning and implementing a budget. It has identified the major items of expenditure associated with living and studying at university and, in the course of this, has provided factual information relating to tuition fees. It has also looked at how university study may be financed, focusing particularly on student loans, student support, taking paid employment whilst studying, and the various options for borrow-ing money. Finally, it has suggested an appropriate approach to managing student finance, which includes useful money-saving tips.

▶ More Feedback . . .

> ❝ One of the biggest changes I had to make when going to univer-sity was my spending awareness. I had to teach myself how to budget for necessities such as food, clothes (and theatre visits!). I really learned the hard way – I ended up living on toast in the spring term because all of my loan had gone on my accommoda-tion and Christmas presents! If I was applying to go to uni again, I think I would want to be encouraged to research the area as well as the uni itself and determine the cost of living, especially because I haven't had the time to do paid work due to the

demands of my degree. The truth is that I have never been able to afford to live here.

(Danielle, 3rd-year undergraduate)

I found it really difficult to manage on my student loan. Everything adds up to so much more than I'd expected. I decided to live in a house in the second year, but I advise students to live back in halls due to financial reasons. I didn't consider the fact that I'd be paying rent over the summer and other holidays which has meant I have to work even when I have essays to do. It has made money really tight this year by living in a house, and I've already advised my sister to apply for halls again in her second year. If you have any money worries your university should have a financial adviser to help you. I had to go to the adviser and she arranged for me to have a short-term loan and apply for an Access to Learning Grant. Don't get more and more worried about money if you are having troubles. Talk to someone and they'll do their best to help.

(Clarissa, 2nd-year undergraduate)

Budgeting has been difficult. Even though I have held down a part-time job for three years, there just doesn't seem to be enough money! Some things have to give – I don't buy that many clothes and I only go out on the weekends. Running a car whilst being at university has been hard, but it is worth it for the inde-pendence and freedom it gives me. I am quite worried about my student loan – the total is something like £13,000–14,000. If I knew how expensive it was going to be I would have saved up for a couple of years before I started university. Unfortunately my parents can't provide me with any financial support, although I don't pay any rent at home and I get all my meals, so I am quite lucky really.

(Louise, 3rd-year undergraduate)

I found that having a part-time job with reasonable hours of 7 hours a week meant that I didn't have to use up all of my student loan in order to pay for things I needed but also didn't have to compromise my study time or social life too much. It's important to balance work, study and going out. Whilst living in halls in the first year my monthly outgoings involved £75 for food, £60 for going out and £25 for my mobile phone bill. This was roughly what I earned working 7 hours a week plus overtime occasionally. This sort of budget doesn't really allow for going out every night but it is a reality I accepted as a part of taking control of my spendings to avoid getting into debt (apart from my student loan), which I think would be much worse than spending a few nights in with a good film and pizza.

,

(**Juliet**, recent graduate)

6 Accommodation

This chapter will focus on finding suitable accommodation. Specifically, it will:

- identify what you need to bear in mind before making your choice
- indicate how you can start your search
- examine the advantages and disadvantages of various types of student accommodation
- provide information about the contract between landlord and tenant
- outline the responsibilities associated with setting up home
- discuss what makes a 'good' housemate

▶ Getting started

In choosing accommodation you will be bound by availability, financial constraints and your own preferences. In terms of the latter point, if you think about your personality, your likes and dislikes, your good points and any bad habits you may have, and relate these to the various lifestyles associated with different types of accommodation, you are more likely to come to the best conclusion as to what is 'right' for you. Here are a few questions to ask yourself:

- ▶ Do you prefer a quiet environment or noise and bustle?
- ▶ Do you value your privacy or does the idea of communal living appeal? To what extent?
- ▶ Would you find sharing a room fun?
- ▶ How much of your free time would you like to spend with other students/non-students?
- ▶ Do you want to live very near to the main university buildings or would you prefer a complete change of environment when you are at home?
- ▶ Do you have any preferences regarding living in a single-sex or mixed environment?

▶ Are you neat or messy, and how important is it that those around you are similar?

▶ Do you have any bad habits or quirks?

▶ Can you think of specific bad habits or lifestyle choices that you would find irritating in others?

▶ Is the idea of independent living attractive or is the prospect of looking after yourself somewhat onerous?

▶ Do you want to do your own catering?

▶ Do you hope to go home in the holidays or do you require accommodation all through the year?

▶ Do you have any special requirements: for example, are you a wheelchair user or do you need somewhere on site to leave a bicycle?

▶ How to start your search

These questions will focus your thoughts and give an indication of the choices that are right for you. The next step is to consider them in the light of what is available at your institution. The first place to start is the university website or prospectus. This will indicate where the halls of residence and student flats are located, the facilities and services on offer and the percentage of the undergraduate population that lives in university accommodation. Most websites also include photographs and maps so that you will be able to determine the distance between the halls and the main buildings and also get a feel for the university layout as a whole.

> ❢ *The worse the accommodation the more fun you have, as you have more money to spend on beer and don't need to worry about wrecking it. Try to get a shared kitchen and bathroom. It's much more sociable and you will meet loads more people.* ❣
> (**William**, 3rd-year undergraduate)

Once you have a basic overview it is wise to contact someone in the accommodation office at your university and arrange to speak to them either on the telephone or in person. This will give you the opportunity to ask further questions and receive supplementary details that may colour your choice. Initially, you need to know the likelihood of being given a place in university accommodation and the criteria for selection, together with the associated costs and details of what is included and excluded. You may need further information that is not available on the website, for example the nature of the facilities on offer and the number of people sharing them, whether the accommodation is for first-year undergraduates only or all students, whether or not it is possible to stay there during the vacations and the associated costs, and details of the frequency and cost of public transport to the main university areas. If some meals are included you need to ascertain which are supplied and which are not, and whether the dining area is actually in the building or at another location. You may need further details such as how the accommodation is heated and the arrangements for cleaning and security. If it is feasible to visit during the summer, this is a good idea as it will enable you to put various options in order of preference and gain a more accurate picture of what it would be like to live in a specific location.

 The one crucial thing to have in your student accommodation is high-speed Internet. It helps for so many reasons.
(**Aaron**, 3rd-year undergraduate)

In addition to exploring the possibilities associated with university accommodation, you need to establish what else is available, together with a sense of the proportion of students taking this option. Most important of all, it is essential to find out what help is offered by the university in terms of finding alternative accommodation. There is likely to be a list of private property available to students and the accommodation office will also know which landlords have to date taken their responsibilities seriously and which are to be avoided. As far as possible it is better to deal with landlords known to your accommodation office. However, if you do need to extend your search you can look in local newspapers that carry accommodation advertisements. Some students contact letting agents but one disadvantage to this is that agents may to be working on commission and, if so, it is in their interest to get the highest possible rent for the landlord. Some may make various charges including a finders' fee, or a fee for checking references and/or drawing up a contract. It is important to check all this and ensure that you are comfortable with the conditions before proceeding. There are good and bad agents and if possible you should use ones belonging the Association of Residential Letting Agents (www.arla.co.uk), or other reputable associations.

It is also worth looking on the university noticeboards as this is where groups of students who need an extra person for their flat-share tend to advertise. Word of mouth works well too, particularly for your second year when you are likely to have a good idea of exactly what you want, together with a wider network of friends and acquaintances. Finding suitable accommodation may not be entirely straightforward, particularly in the private sector, and the best way of avoiding the pitfalls is to ensure that you find out the basics about renting (see over), think about the complexities involved and reflect on what you think is right for you before actually signing a contract. Talking to the accommodation officer will enable him or her to gain an impression of your preferences, give you relevant and appropriate advice and more easily match your requirements to what is available. Moreover, time is of the essence in view of the large numbers of students requiring accommodation, so it is a good idea to establish contact as soon as possible.

> ❛ *The accommodation was pretty dreary but I did have a large pinboard in my room which I pinned all my 'good luck' cards to.* ❜
> (**Abi**, 1st-year undergraduate)

▶ Types of accommodation

There are many different types of student accommodation and, unsurprisingly, large variations in price and availability in different parts of the country. As soon as you know where you will be studying, you should contact the accommodation office at the university for an overview. It is preferable to try to sort out your accommodation as soon as possible after you have confirmed your place. Once you are living there, you will be in a position to find out more about general availability, and you might also meet third-year undergraduates who intend to vacate their own accommodation in time for you to take it on. If you intend to live out in your second year, you should keep your eyes and ears open from the outset, but be aware that to confirm a definite interest in a property you may have to start paying rent earlier than you would wish in order to secure it for yourself. Therefore the best time to begin looking seriously is after the Easter break when the property is likely to be occupied until the summer vacation at least. In very broad terms, it is often cheaper to rent a room in hall than a room in a private flat, and cheaper still to live with a family. Circumstances vary, and it is important to make a choice that is right for you.

Halls of residence
Halls of residence are generally purpose-built blocks comprising large numbers of study bedrooms each of which is furnished with a bed, a desk, a wardrobe, shelving and storage, with shared bathroom facilities down the corridor. However, from this basic blueprint there are many variations; for example, some rooms may accommodate two students sharing and others may even have en-suite facilities. Catering facilities vary from hall to hall: some may offer all or some catered meals in a dining area; others may provide a fully equipped kitchen that may be shared by a certain number of

students. The facilities available are likely to affect the level of fees – for example, it is normally much cheaper to share a room. Halls tend to be run by a warden, supported by a committee of students. Although there are usually few rules, the presence of the warden does mean that students with grievances do have someone to whom they can turn. Most rules tend to focus on deterring antisocial behaviour such as noise nuisance, but others may prohibit overnight guests. It is very important that you are aware of the rules and are willing to comply with them before opting to live in a hall.

 I hate living in halls – noisy first years!
(**Katy**, 3rd-year undergraduate)

For many new undergraduates, a hall of residence is a good choice for the first year, mainly because it offers the opportunity to meet many new people who are all in the same position of being in a new environment. If you are feeling homesick or lonely and want to talk to someone, it is very likely that in a hall environment you can bump into other students in the corridor or in the bar if there is one. Moreover, it eliminates the need to go house hunting, which can be difficult for people new to the area and to the university. There are also other advantages: halls of residence tend to be well heated, and maintenance problems are usually dealt with swiftly, and generally do not involve the students. Security is normally good, and most halls are staffed by cleaners who will clean each study bedroom once a week in addition to the communal areas. The hall fees may seem steep at first glance but may actually represent a cheaper alternative to renting privately, which has many hidden costs. Moreover, another advantage to living in hall is that you do not pay for your room during the summer vacation.

 The only bad thing about halls is the fact you don't get to choose who you live with. It means you get stuck with at least one crazy person for a year.
(**Anne**, 3rd-year undergraduate)

However, there are disadvantages: halls tend to be noisy, with students arriving and departing at all hours, and you may not particularly like the people living near you. You may have a problem using shared facilities as people have different standards of hygiene and cleanliness, so you may need to clean up before you use them even if it is not your mess. You may not like the food that is provided or, if you are self-catering, you may find that the kitchen is very congested at mealtimes. You may also find that food you have put in the communal fridge disappears without trace just when you want to eat it. The location of the hall may not suit you either, particularly if, for example, you prefer to work in the library on some evenings and the hall is some distance from the main university buildings. You will probably have to vacate your room at the end of each term (and remove all your things), as it may be used for conference accommodation in the holidays.

> ❛ *Practically, the hardest bit was having to upheave all my belongings to my 'new home' and to take them back again every holiday. You are never completely settled. In my second and third years it was so much better to have a 'proper home'.* ❜
>
> (**Suzanne**, 3rd-year undergraduate)

Student cluster flats/houses/villages

Many universities now provide purpose-built accommodation arranged in student flats, houses or villages. Each individual flat or house is designed to meet the needs of small groups of students, but there are usually several flats or houses on the same site, often arranged in blocks. In a sense this type of accommodation may be viewed as a bridge between a room in hall and a privately rented flat. A typical cluster flat might have six to eight bedrooms with shared kitchen and bathroom facilities. The key to an individual room may also open the main door to the flat thus restricting access to the six or so residents. This accommodation tends to be very popular, particularly with second- and third-year students, because it enables groups of friends to live together with a good balance between privacy and independence. With fewer people sharing the facilities it is immediately apparent if someone does not pull their weight in terms of household chores, or if anyone has the habit of using other people's food. If you are living with people you like, it can feel like a home from home, but equally, if there are personality clashes, it is more difficult to ignore them.

> ❛ *I was put in university flats and found it difficult to meet people at first as not much was organised for the people living there.* ❜
>
> (**Rakesh**, 3rd-year undergraduate)

At some universities students are expected to be responsible for keeping the accommodation clean whereas at others a weekly cleaner is provided. Also, the equipment provided varies from one institution to another. If you are assigned to a cluster flat or house you should ascertain what equipment you would need to supply yourself and enquire about arrangements for cleaning, maintenance and reporting complaints.

My first-year accommodation was fine although inevitably there was one flatmate amongst the five of us who just did not mix well. He left his washing-up for two weeks and eventually it grew mould. Because we hated him we put it all back in his cupboard and it stayed there throughout the Christmas holidays – about a month! Ugh!

(**Laura**, 3rd-year undergraduate)

Private-sector halls of residence

In some parts of the country, particularly London, Manchester and Liverpool, some organisations such as housing associations have constructed purpose-built accommodation for students, nurses and others. In recent years expansion in this sector has been considerable and they are likely to be one of the principal providers of student housing in the future. Private halls tend to be more expensive than university halls of residence but often have good facilities such as en-suite arrangements. This type of accommodation may suit students who wish to live with a mix of people from within and outside the university. However, there have been problems, most particularly that some halls are being built to open at the start of a new academic year, yet they fail to meet the completion date. The NUS and other interested bodies have set up a Code of Standards in response. Students considering taking up a place in a private hall are advised to check whether or not the company concerned is signed up to this, prior to proceeding. Further information may be found on www.unipol.leeds.ac.uk/largercode/.

Hostels

Hostels provide reasonably priced accommodation, normally comprising shared bathroom facilities and a shared room at first with the possibility of a single room later on. They may offer partial board or self-catering arrangements and variable contract lengths. Whilst many hostels are available only to students, others accept people working in the area in question, and it is often possible to remain in residence during the summer vacation. The attractiveness of a particular hostel may well depend on who else stays there and its location in relation to the university. As with other types of communal accommodation, there is likely to be a long waiting list.

Private flat/house share

Many students opt to share a flat or a house with their friends, or to rent a room in a house with others. Sometimes the landlord lives on site too. If renting in the private sector is your preferred choice, you need to think initially about the type of accommodation you require, how much you can afford to pay for it, who you will be living with and the location. Whereas if you live in a hall of residence your costs will probably be inclusive of bills, if you share a flat you are likely to have to pay a percentage of all bills on top of your rent. It is therefore very important to bear this in mind before making your final choice. You can always ask to see previous utility bills if you wish to ascertain a fairly accurate estimate of your likely expenditure. In terms of the location, the key points to bear in mind are your personal safety and the travel costs. You need to ensure that you are comfortable with the journey between home and university as you may need to make this journey alone and late at night. Check the bus routes and the frequency of services as this may affect your decision. Note the route and the distance to the closest supermarket and other local facilities as this is another journey you may frequently have to undertake. It may be cheaper to live further away from the university but you should consider this in the light of the travel costs you may incur.

 Don't live in campus-owned accommodation. Private is a lot more fun – lax rules and more parties.
(Den, 1st-year undergraduate)

Be prepared to be asked for references or a guarantor's name and address by your future landlord. If you have rented before you should ask your previous landlord for a reference, or, if this is your second year and you spent the first in hall, you could ask for a letter from the university confirming that there were no problems and that you paid your fees on time. If you have no history of renting at all, you may need to provide a reference from your bank and to ask your parents to act as guarantors.

Visiting potential properties
In terms of the property itself, you should look at the general state of repair and note anything that concerns you. If you decide to proceed, your landlord may agree, in the course of your negotiations, to make certain improvements prior to your moving in. However, beware properties in very poor condition. If the roof looks as if it is in a poor state of repair or the timbers are rotten, you may wish to reconsider. Look for signs of rot, damp and leaks and note the state of the window frames. Check how the property is heated and, if you are visiting in the summer, try to imagine whether or not it would be adequate in the winter. Ensure that there are sufficient kitchen, bathroom and communal facilities for the number of people in the house, and ascertain whether or not the plumbing (lavatories, taps etc.) and appliances (cooker,

fridge etc.) appear to be working. Your safety and security is paramount and, as indicated below, your landlord has certain legal undertakings in this regard. When you visit, check the fire precautions such as a fire escape, fire doors, fire extinguishers and smoke alarms and think about whether or not the layout of the dwelling would allow for straightforward evacuation in the event of a fire.

Look at the number and state of repair of the plug points in each room and the general condition of the electrical wiring, and note whether or not there are access points to the Internet. Check if there are window locks and whether the locks on the front door are adequate. Ask the landlord if you can see a current inspection certificate for any gas appliances and check that the person who carried it out was CORGI registered. Ask whether the wiring has been checked recently and to see any documentation that supports this, and enquire whether the soft furnishings comply with fire regulations. (Since landlords are aware of this requirement many retain the relevant labels on the furniture as proof.) If possible, talk to a current tenant and ask about residual or recurring problems. If there is a garden, ask whether or not you would be entitled to use it and, if so, whether the maintenance would be your responsibility. Ask about the neighbours and any problems, for example with noise, in recent years. Finally, it is not unreasonable to ask for proof that your landlord either owns the property or has the owner's permission to rent it out to you. You should ideally come to a verbal agreement with the landlord about what is expected from all parties as this can then be reflected in a written contract, which is essential in terms of minimising subsequent problems and misunderstandings.

> ‘ *Second-year accommodation is harder to come by and depend-ing on which let company you choose, can seem unfair. I lived in a seven-bedroom house which practically fell apart through the year. Plumbing, heating, water – all disrupted regularly. For this house the rate was £50 per week including bills. Satisfactory? Another house down the road – seven bedrooms, fully refur-bished – £46 per week! Can be difficult!* ’
>
> (**Max**, 3rd-year undergraduate)

The contract

Before you sign any written contract, read it carefully and make sure that you understand it. If you don't, ask your accommodation officer to check it for you, or ask for help from your local Citizen's Advice Bureau (branch details available from www.nacab.org.uk) or Shelter (website www.shelter.org.uk or advice line 0808 800444). Do not take anything for granted; seek clarification if necessary and ensure that you understand your responsibilities fully. Put as much as possible in writing, such as how long you will live in the property, with start and end dates; your rent; the arrangements concerning when and how it will be paid; your financial responsibilities should another tenant leave; your rights, if any, in the event of a new tenant being chosen; how an inventory will be taken and by whom; the arrangements regarding any deposit required by the landlord and the conditions under which money can be withheld by him or her; the arrangements with regard to repairs; the appropriate time-scale in which repairs should be carried out, and a precise account of the landlord's responsibilities and your responsibilities. If you rent a room in a property, ensure that you know with whom you will be sharing, that is, whether they are students or other individuals, and whether they include your landlord. In all cases, make sure that you have your landlord's name and address and that you are able to contact him or her in an emergency.

Your legal rights differ depending on the type of contract you have. This is a very complex issue and if you have any doubts it is wise to take advice from your accommodation officer. (Housing law in Scotland is different, and students in Scotland can find further information by clicking 'Scotland' on Shelter's website, www.shelter.org.uk.) Most tenancy agreements are assured shorthold tenancies in which each individual sharing the property is responsible for paying his or her own rent. The legal position in this instance is that tenants have the right to remain in the property for six months, or for a longer fixed term defined at the outset. If you do not have a fixed-term agreement the landlord can give you notice to leave after the initial six months. The main disadvantage to this form of contract is that if somebody leaves earlier than planned you do not have any rights in choosing their replacement. Another disadvantage is that each person sharing will need an individual television licence. If you have a joint tenancy agreement you are jointly responsible for paying the rent, which means that if somebody leaves everyone else is responsible for making up the shortfall in rent until another tenant can be found. Your contract may also position you as an excluded occupier, for example if you share accommodation with your landlord, and in this event you will have fewer legal rights. It is difficult to generalise about contract agreements and each one should be read individually. If anything is unclear it is wise to seek advice before signing it. In addition to the afore-mentioned sites of advice and information, relevant publications containing essential advice and recommendations may also be obtained from several sources: the Office of Fair Trading (website www.oft.gov.uk or telephone 0870 60 60 321 [mailing house]) or [helpline] 08457 22 44 99) publishes 'Guidance on Unfair Terms in Tenancy Agreements'; the ODPM, Office of the Deputy Prime Minister, has produced a booklet entitled 'Assured and

Assured Shorthold Tenancies. A Guide for Tenants' (available by telephoning 0870 1226 236), and the Legal Services Commission has published a leaflet, 'Renting and Letting – Rights for Landlords and Tenants' (available by telephoning 0845 3000 343).

The landlord's responsibilities

Legislation, including the Landlord and Tenant Act 1985, is in place to protect the tenant. The issue of the landlord's responsibilities is a complex one but, basically, she or he must ensure that the property is kept in a good state of repair and take certain specific measures to protect the health and safety of the tenant. The landlord's responsibilities include ensuring that the structure of the building is sound and that if the water supply, sewage system or heating develop faults, that repairs are carried out within a reasonable time-scale. Gas appliances must be inspected every twelve months by a CORGI-registered engineer and a safety certificate issued, and soft furnishings have to meet strict fire regulations. In addition to this, landlords are generally responsible for providing adequate locks, smoke detectors and rubbish bins, ensuring that there is adequate storage space for refuse and that all common parts are kept clear, and maintaining the property to the same standard as it was at the beginning of the tenancy. If the landlord does not live at the property, he or she is still entitled to inspect it from time to time having given due notice, and also to gain access in order to carry out repairs or for other essential reasons.

The tenant's responsibilities

A good tenant pays rent promptly and in full, adheres to the terms of the lease at all times, ensures that the property is kept in good order, looks after the appliances and equipment provided and does not cause problems in terms of damaging the property in any way or creating noise nuisance. It is the tenant's responsibility to repair or replace anything that he or she personally breaks or damages.

Avoiding problems

To date, one of the key problems for tenants has been recovering the deposit, although it is hoped that the new Tenancy Deposit Protection Scheme will help in this regard in the future. From the tenant's perspective, the main protection lies in taking precautions against problems at the outset. On arrival, a detailed and thorough inventory and schedule of condition of the flat should be taken and signed by all parties. In terms of the inventory, absolutely every item that is included in the flat, from large pieces of furniture to small kitchen utensils, should be listed. The schedule of condition should include notes about the condition of each room, noting any stains on the carpets, tears in the curtains, damage to the walls, cigarette burns, cracks in the tiles and so on. Notes should be taken about the standard of cleanliness of the paintwork and, wherever possible, photographs should be taken, preferably with a record of the date on the film.

If your landlord is unavailable or unwilling to check these documents and sign them, ask an independent witness to do so and post the landlord a copy by registered mail. A few weeks before you are due to vacate the property you should clean it as thoroughly as possible and check the condition of the flat and the contents against your original inventory. It is also wise to take another set of dated photographs as evidence. Towards the end of the tenancy, arrange for your landlord to visit and assess the flat in good time to enable you to carry out any small repairs (not wear and tear, for which you are not liable), that she or he may consider to be your responsibility and arrange for the landlord to call again on your day of departure to ensure that all necessary works have been carried out. Return the keys and write asking for your deposit to be returned. Some landlords will also require evidence that all the utility bills have been paid to date.

 Bring personal items with you to make it feel like home. Try and keep things clean and tidy otherwise you will lose your deposit.
(**Charlie**, 3rd-year undergraduate)

Throughout your tenancy try to keep a line of communication open with your landlord. This will help you if anything breaks down as he or she will be able to keep you notified of progress. If you break anything, tell your landlord immediately and, similarly, if you anticipate difficulties in paying your rent on time, tell the landlord and try to make mutually convenient alternative arrangements. It is best to put all communication in writing and to obtain receipts for all sums of money paid out. If you have a good relationship with your landlord you are likely to have fewer problems. If the relationship becomes progressively difficult, or you face major problems such as eviction or harassment, you may wish to seek advice from either your accommodation officer or from outside organisations such as Shelter or the Citizen's Advice Bureau.

Housing Act 2004

In November 2004 a new Housing Bill received Royal Assent and the bulk of its reforms will be implemented by the end of 2006. Students are likely to benefit from many of its provisions, notably the Tenancy Deposit Protection arrangements (a new Government-sponsored scheme which will safeguard tenancy deposits); the drive to introduce greater regulation of estate agents; the improved controls on Housing in Multiple Occupation (HMOs), which include a mandatory national licensing scheme aiming to raise the long-term quality of dwellings; Selective Licensing, to ensure that bad landlords take more responsibility for managing their properties and dealing with the associated issues; and the establishment of a new Housing Health and Safety Rating System (HHSRS), to assist councils in targeting properties in the worst condition.

Lodgings

Some students opt to rent a room within a family home, sharing the bathroom and kitchen facilities with the family. The cost is likely to vary according to the location of the house, the size of the room and the facilities provided, but this is generally a cheaper option than renting a room in a shared flat, particularly as bills are quite often included in the rent. This type of accommodation may suit undergraduates who wish to have some respite from the student scene when they get home or who are happiest living in a family environment. It may also appeal because the standard of upkeep is usually higher in owner-occupied residences. However, some students may feel lonely away from their friends and they may also find it inhibiting to live by someone else's rules. There may, for example, be limitations on the numbers of guests that may be invited back to the room and the times during which visitors are permitted.

Living at home

 I stayed at home. I feel I missed out on the whole 'living in halls' thing. It seemed to me that other students had already built a sense of community before the course had started, through living in halls.

(**Bill**, 3rd-year undergraduate)

Some students continue to live with their parents throughout their university years. The main advantage to this is that it does not incur heavy accommodation costs. The change of lifestyle is initially less significant for undergraduates who live at home, as, unlike their counterparts who may be feeling homesick or apprehensive, these students are living in familiar and comfortable surroundings. However, the key disadvantage is that students may feel that they are not getting the most out of the university experience. This may particularly be the case if the student has to travel some distance to university.

> ❝ *I currently commute to uni [from home]. Getting on that train for the first time was very nerve-wracking. I did a dummy run the week before so I knew where I was going. I really enjoy uni. Travelling is not as much of a chore as it seems. It's a great opportunity to get my masses of reading done!* ❞
>
> (**Helena**, 1st-year undergraduate)

If you choose to live at home it is important that you make an effort to participate in university life as much as is possible. Joining clubs and societies will help, as will making a conscious effort to socialise with other students. You may also find it helpful to become more independent at home, particularly if to date your parents have taken responsibility for all your cooking, washing and cleaning requirements. If you try to be more autonomous you will have more in common with your peers and will be making useful preparations for eventually leaving home after university. It is a good time to negotiate any necessary new arrangements with your parents to reflect that you are now responsible for co-ordinating your own study and social commitments. You may also need to give some thought to the layout of your study bedroom, and to acquire extra furniture that may help you to organise your work (if you don't already have them), such as a desk, bookcase and filing cabinet.

> ❝ *Although I wanted to live in the uni halls I was told that I lived too close to apply. The uni offered to find a place in a shared home but this idea didn't appeal to me much as I would not know the people I would be sharing with and didn't feel comfortable with that. In the end I decided just to stay at home.* ❞
>
> (**Sunita**, 1st-year undergraduate)

Specific Circumstances

If your circumstances mean that you have specific requirements in terms of accommodation, for example that you have a disability, or that you are a single parent, it is essential to draw this to the attention of your accommodation officer as soon as possible. Unfortunately, universities tend to make little provision for students with families, although some housing associations and hostels may be able to help. Facilities for disabled students vary from institution to institution and it is a matter of finding the best match for your requirements. If you decide to rent in the private sector, you can obtain more information about your rights from the DRC (Disability Rights Commission) on www.drc.org.uk. Students with disabilities may also find it useful to contact the housing department of the local council and investigate the possibility of council housing.

▶ Responsibilities

There are many responsibilities associated with setting up your own home, whether it is in a hall of residence or a privately rented flat. All students need to insure their belongings and ensure that they have an appropriate television licence. In addition, those renting in the private sector need to advise all the utility companies that they are now responsible for the property in question and make arrangements to pay the appropriate bills.

TV licence

If you take a television to university you will need a licence as this will not be covered by licences held by your parents or the university. Also, students sharing a flat or house should not assume that they only need one licence for all televisions as this depends on the tenancy agreement. It is wise to check the rules (www.tv-l.co.uk) to avoid prosecution and a large fine. You can obtain a form for a TV licence from a Post Office.

Insurance

It is unwise to regard insurance as unnecessary expenditure. Some students may be covered by their parents' policy, but most are not. A good place to start is Endsleigh (www.endsleigh.co.uk), as this organisation specialises in insurance for students. It is tailor-made to suit the individual student's needs and can cover damage to landlords' property and legal expenses in addition to personal possessions.

Utility companies

If you rent a flat or house, you need to advise the utility companies (gas, electricity, water and telephone) that you are now responsible for the bills. You will be able to get the relevant names and addresses from the landlord. Ensure that the meters are read before you move in, and if you are uncertain as to whether or not this has been done, note the meter readings on your arrival and send this information to the providers. You may have to pay an initial deposit for some utilities. It is not normally possible to put all tenants' names on the bill, and, even if it is, the person who requests the new account is likely to be considered by the utility companies as the legal account holder and therefore the person responsible for the bill. It is very, very important that before agreeing to rent a property all the tenants concerned are clear about their responsibilities with regard to the bills. Whilst in theory this agreement could be outlined in a legal document between occupants, in practice it is normally only agreed verbally and based on mutual trust and, unfortunately, problems do sometimes arise. Moreover, if one or more tenant does not pay his or her share of the bill, the others may feel obliged to make up the shortfall whilst the problem is sorted out – otherwise, if the bills are not paid, the utility may be cut off and the provider may instigate a civil action for debt against the relevant party. One option might be for each tenant to put her or his name on one bill as a gesture of goodwill. This does not absolve the others of their responsibilities but it is an active way of demonstrating a shared commitment. Another option might be for each occupant to give the named account holder a deposit to guard against a potential future liability. Repayment meters for gas and electricity may also be a possibility although this option is likely to require the landlord's consent.

It is worth bearing in mind that most problems stem from the telephone bill, which can quickly become very large despite each individual being convinced that he or she has only made a few calls. It is a good idea to think in advance about what might be done to prevent this, particularly if everyone concerned already owns a mobile phone. Some telephone providers will, for a one-off fee, limit the line to receiving incoming calls only, or bar overseas and premium-rate outgoing calls. Alternatively, most providers will issue itemised bills. However, it can be very time-consuming to sort out who owes what, and people may not remember who made specific calls, so it may still not be possible to account for the source of all calls.

Council Tax

Full-time students are exempt from Council Tax. However, if students are renting with non-students or part-time students in a shared flat or house, there will be a Council Tax bill for the property. If you are in this situation it is essential that before entering into any agreement you decide whether the bill will only be split between those ineligible for exemption or whether all members of the household will be expected to help. Legally you do not have to pay, but it would be a good idea to check that your fellow flatmates also see it this way.

▶ Finding compatible flatmates/housemates

Many students enjoy living in small groups in a shared flat or house. However, if the arrangement is to work well, it is essential that housemates are compatible. It is not sufficient simply to choose people you like. They may have habits that you find irritating, which over time may become intolerable. The best course of action is to think very carefully about what you want and what you don't want, and to draw up some mutually acceptable guidelines before embarking on a flat- or house-share. It is essential to be honest: most disagreements stem from one party feeling that another is taking advantage of them. Common causes of tension include one person feeling that he or she is paying for more than is reasonable, or bearing the brunt of the cleaning, cooking or shopping duties.

> ❝ *What I have learned is that people can change over time. In the first year, four people can get on fantastically well, but now in the third year it is becoming almost unbearable. Girlfriends etc. practically moving in can disrupt and cause conflicts between other housemates: gas/water/electricity bills etc. not being paid for or going over the limit, due to an extra person using the amenities.* ❞
>
> (**Peter**, 3rd-year undergraduate)

In the first instance you should decide whether you want to live with people of the same gender or in a mixed household, and, ideally, with how many people you would like to share. Next, focus on all the potential pitfalls that you would like to avoid, thinking particularly about your own attitudes to cleanliness, noise, tidiness and guests. Be aware that even if you are very easy-going, some of your own habits may not go down well with your friends. Ask yourself and your potential flatmates the following questions. If there are significant discrepancies in your answers, it is likely that problems would arise were you to share. Try to pick people with compatible views to your own:

> ❝ *I hope that the people I live with have a decent standard of hygiene etc. I suppose that's one thing I'm fearful of – not having the right people sharing accommodation with me.* ❞
>
> (**Veer**, sixth-former)

- ▶ Do you all agree about how long you want to rent for, that is, what constitutes the most appropriate length of lease?
- ▶ Do you smoke? Do you mind if others around you smoke?
- ▶ What time do you like to go to sleep, and do you mind if others are playing music past this time?
- ▶ Do you like to study in a quiet environment or do you prefer to listen to your music while you study?
- ▶ Are you likely to invite overnight guests to the flat? How frequently? Would it irritate you if others often had overnight guests? Do you think overnight guests should make a contribution to the food bills?

► How are you intending to divide up the bills? Will you each buy your own food or will you share? What about the basics, such as milk? Who will cook?

► If you intend to be jointly responsible for the heating bill, would you be happy to pay an equal share even if you are out all day and others are working from home with the heating on?

► How will you divide the telephone bill? If you decide to have a box for money next to the telephone, what would you do if the contents did not cover the bill?

► Are you all students, and therefore exempt from Council Tax? If not, will the non-student(s) divide the Council Tax that is due between themselves?

► Are you planning to have a cleaning roster? How frequently do you think the flat should be cleaned?

► If you have made a mess in, for example, the kitchen, what would you consider to be a reasonable time-scale for clearing it up?

► How tidy are you? How do you feel about untidiness in others?

► Will breakages be regarded as a communal cost?

► Will you each do your own shopping or will you shop communally?

► If you have a kitty for communal expenses, which items should be purchased from this kitty?

► What would happen if one person were to leave, both in terms of the finances and finding a replacement?

The key to a successful arrangement is to discuss these and other issues with your potential flatmates. You should then write out what you have decided the 'house rules' will be so as to avoid any misunderstandings later. If you decide to shop separately, try to assign different shelves and cupboard space to each individual. If you have a communal kitty for basics, check that you are all clear about what it covers and what it does not. Ensure that you have reached agreement regarding cleaning and tidying the flat, overnight guests and playing loud music. Be sensitive to how others may interpret your actions: if you constantly 'borrow' milk or other food from the fridge for your own use and never replace it, this is likely to irritate those who have taken the trouble to buy it. There is nothing worse than coming home from lectures, opening the fridge and finding that the food you had bought for your evening meal has gone. Similarly, if you put off your cleaning duties until others feel compelled to clean up on your behalf, this will lead to problems. And if you have decided to divide the telephone bill equally and one person's usage is higher than everyone else's, this may lead to resentment. It is very, very important to be honest and open when you are formulating the house rules. There is nothing wrong with opting to shop separately if you think that sharing will cause problems.

> ❦ *Choose carefully and be prepared for menial 'Mum' matters such as buying toilet roll to suddenly become serious issues! Discover the wonders of carpet cleaner on red wine!*
> (**Kerry**, 3rd-year undergraduate)

If, once you are living together, you find that an individual's behaviour is irritating you, try to tackle it sensitively by talking to the person concerned early on in as light-hearted a manner as possible. Do not leave it to fester and grow. If the flat-share works, it is likely to be a very fulfilling and enjoyable experience. Indeed, many students look back on their flat-sharing days as one of the highlights of life at university.

▶ Summary

This chapter has looked at the various accommodation options available to students. It has identified the advantages and disadvantages of each and offered guidance on making an appropriate choice. It has indicated what students should look for when renting and examined the responsibilities of both landlords and tenants. Having outlined what is involved in setting up home, it has also looked at the issue of finding compatible flatmates.

▶ More Feedback . . .

> ❦ *Being at university, the one thing that has made it easier to cope was my choice of living arrangements. I chose the halls of residence because of the social value and experience. It was difficult at first to adjust to having to do things for myself and to be totally surrounded by people. There are downsides, however, as the noise and mess can be unbearable at times, but I have learnt already to respect others and the flat.*
> (**Carol**, 1st-year undergraduate)

> ❦ *In the first year I chose to live in a self-catering university flat rather than halls. I found that I didn't meet as many people as I probably would have done in halls. On the other hand, I had fun with my flatmates and really had a chance to get to know them*

well, which I think can be more difficult in halls. Also I appreciated the independence that I got from being able to cook whatever I wanted whenever I was hungry.

(**Henrietta**, 3rd-year undergraduate)

I chose to live in halls in the first year and I'm really glad I made this decision. The social life in halls is great because you see so many people every day. In houses it requires more effort to see people often. Living in a house in the second year was great in a different way but this depends very much on your housemates. I was really lucky with mine. They are five of the greatest people I know.

(**John**, 2nd-year undergraduate)

I chose my university for two reasons: firstly, it offered the course I wanted to do, and secondly, because it is within travelling distance of my parents' house. (I didn't want the financial burden of moving out.) I did decide to move out in the second year because I was finding the bus and train journeys very tiring. I moved in with one other person. The downside was that I had to increase my student loan to cover my extra costs which I wasn't very happy about. I found that living away from home made me more confident and independent, and I learned how to cook! I'm glad I did it; however, it was so expensive that I made the decision to move back home for my final year. I had started driving by then so would not have the worry about getting the train.

(**Louise**, 3rd-year undergraduate)

7 Studying at University

This chapter will look at how to study successfully at university. It will:

- identify the differences between sixth form/college and university study
- focus on the teaching structure of lectures, seminars, field research and tutorials and give guidelines on how to gain the most from them
- show how you can use the university's facilities to your advantage
- give guidelines on how to study effectively
- analyse forms of assessment and their requirements
- offer advice on dealing with problems associated with your studies

▶ First impressions of university study

Studying at university is very different from college or sixth form study, and most students will experience something of a culture shock when they first arrive. Everything is on a larger scale, with more staff, more students and more going on. From being a large fish in a small pond, it may be somewhat overwhelming to be one of over a hundred undergraduates in a lecture theatre, facing unknown topics, new terminology and jargon, lengthy booklists, a timetable that initially seems complex and different from everyone else's, a far greater number of staff than you may have encountered previously, and all this within a totally new and unfamiliar geographical location. However, the main difference is likely to be the recognition that you are no longer going to be spoon-fed: from now on it will be up to you whether or not you attend lectures, tutorials and so on, whether or not you hand in your work on time, how much effort you put into background research and reading around your subject, and when and where you do your work. From being expected to produce short pieces of work every day or so, you may now have a deadline that is several weeks away, but the work involved may be considerable and include wide reading, research and analysis. In addition, you are likely to be expected to plan and undertake your work with few external guidelines and far less supervision than you may have experienced at school or college. In short, you will now be treated as an adult: the environment and facilities to enable you to study will be supplied but the motivation and self-discipline must come from you.

> *The transition from sixth form to university was majorly different. The ways in which the classes operate now give me more time to study and prepare for assignments and tests.*
>
> (**Nazneen**, 1st-year undergraduate)

Initially, many students feel a little overwhelmed by their first impressions of the scale of the study that lies ahead. This is a very normal reaction, and the best response is to think about all the component parts of university study and gradually work out how you can use the resources available to achieve the best results. If you keep track of what you need to do and the deadlines associated with each task, and work steadily to a plan, you will find that you make progress. This chapter will help by analysing the learning environment and indicating how you can study most effectively within it.

> *There is a huge difference between studying at university and High School-based education [including] finding and dealing with different sources of materials (journals, books, electronic databases etc.). All of the above take time and a certain degree of trial and error to get used to.*
>
> (**Richard**, 3rd-year undergraduate)

▶ The university timetable

The teaching structure at university is based on a combination of lectures, practical tasks such as fieldwork or laboratory work, seminars and tutorials. These form the framework of the courses, but in addition students are expected to spend a considerable time reading around each topic, writing appropriate assignments and presentations and undertaking further research and investigation when necessary. University study is open-ended in so far as there are always more books to read and more research to do. Since courses generally comprise several modules, all with these implicit demands, the prospect of coping with the workload can at first seem very daunting. However, if you organise and plan your work well and use your time wisely you will soon find that you start to build up your knowledge of your subject.

At first you will develop areas of expertise centring on individual modules which increase your knowledge in specific areas, but as the months progress these will merge and you should begin to achieve a comprehensive view of your subject as a whole.

> ❛ *Studying at school is much easier as time management is controlled by teachers. The freedom of self-teaching is very challenging. The impersonal atmosphere in some courses is difficult and one-to-one, very limited.*
>
> (**Jon**, 3rd-year undergraduate)

In order to make the most of the study opportunities at university it is very important to be organised from the outset to ensure that you attend all the lectures, seminars and tutorials required, and that you also set aside sufficient time for private study. The first step is to draw up a timetable to include all your study commitments. It is not sufficient to try to remember this and carry a mental map in your head – you need several copies of a written version so that you can keep one in your room, one in your bag and one in your computer. Once you have plotted your study commitments it will be easier to see where the gaps are and where you can slot in any paid work arrangements; when you can set aside time for private study; and when you can socialise or devote time to hobbies, sport and other extra-curricular activities. You may find it helpful to purchase a good planner or diary (such as *The Palgrave Student Planner* [46]) as an alternative to designing your own.

Organisation and planning are also key to maximising the value of lectures, seminars, fieldwork and tutorials, and if you are adequately prepared for them you will find it easier to learn and increase your knowledge base.

Lectures

Lectures are an essential part of the university learning structure as they map out the central issues associated with a topic. Typically, one person will address a large group of students on a given subject for approximately an hour. Although there may be a few minutes for questions at the end, there is not normally much opportunity for debate. The lecturer is there to impart knowledge and provide an outline for further study, and the student's role is to listen and write summary notes to which he or she can later refer. Some students find it daunting to be in a large room with people they do not know, listening to detailed information about a new topic delivered at a speed at which it is not possible to write everything down. However, although the situation may seem new and unfamiliar, it does not take long to learn how to maximise learning from lectures.

Firstly, ensure that you have the appropriate equipment with you. This should include plenty of writing paper and a couple of pens, a highlighter pen, and a folder for handouts and completed notes. As the lecture series progresses, you should allocate a specific file to each subject. At first it may be possible to carry the subject files around with you, but as they get heavier you may prefer the system of keeping a 'pending' folder in your bag into which you can place any new handouts, lecture notes and so on, and then filing all your notes in the appropriate places when you return to your room at the end of each day. It is worth being disciplined about this, as it only takes five minutes if undertaken regularly, whereas sorting out a semester's or a term's worth of assorted notes is a major task.

> *Go to as many of your lectures/seminars as you can. As long as you turn up the first year is easy.*
>
> (**Mike**, 3rd-year undergraduate)

Secondly, bear in mind that you are not taking dictation! You are listening to the lecturer's ideas and taking notes, so concentrate on the themes and thoughts expressed and do not try to copy down phrases verbatim. Don't worry about writing in complete sentences as this is not necessary: just try to ensure that you jot down the main points, and use your own personal short-hand if this helps. Make sure that you will be able to identify your notes easily by using the time before the lecture starts to write down the title of the lecture, the module, the speaker and the date. Leave a few lines after that, so that at the end of the lecture you can spend a few minutes writing a very brief summary of what has been discussed. Indeed, leave frequent gaps throughout your notes, so that you can add details later if necessary. If you can bear to spend a little time immediately after the lecture re-reading what you have written and filling in any blanks, this will ensure that when you return to your notes at a later date they will make sense. Similarly, using a highlighter pen to indicate the key points will also help you later. Do not attempt to tape record your lectures. Many universities do not allow this, but even if recording is permitted you should hesitate from doing so because you will simply create more work for yourself in that you will have to listen to the lecture all over again in real time and take notes. Don't worry if you are not good at picking out the salient points when you begin attending lectures – this is a skill that you will acquire with perseverance.

> *It is great being able to study your subject in a university environ-ment – learning and exploring so many new ideas and theories and considering things you have never thought of before.*
>
> (**Rose**, 1st-year undergraduate)

All lecturers have their own style of delivery and you will find some easier to follow than others. You may also find that some lectures are punctuated by new terms and jargon that initially you do not understand. If these recur, jot them down on a separate piece of paper and look them up in the dictionary later. It is important not to ignore them as you may be expected to demonstrate your understanding of this specialist language by reflecting the terms in your assignments. If you look them up at the beginning and hear them in lectures and seminars they will soon become part of your own thought processes.

You are perfectly within your rights to e-mail the lecturer if you need clarification on a specific point, or if, for example, you need help in navigating the reading list. Most lecturers provide a long reading list, not particularly because it is essential to read every book on it, but because they are aware that many students will be chasing a few library copies, so they widen the list to allow students more choice. It is not always essential to read the entire book: it may suffice to skim through it and focus on a particular chapter or section.

Make sure that you attend all your lectures, even if you have not had time to read anything or prepare in any way. It is surprising how much you may recall at a later date, and how much the content of lectures will contribute to your overall understanding of the subject. Also, it is likely that end-of-year examinations may be based on the lecture series and even possible that the lecturer will set the paper. You cannot afford to miss hints and guidance on the salient points of specific topics and how they might be handled, so do not be tempted to miss lectures under any circumstances.

Seminars

A seminar is the name given to a small discussion group comprising typically between three and twelve students and mediated by a tutor. The key purpose of a seminar is to allow students to express their views and interpretations of a specific topic and the relevant literature or research findings. If lectures are the means of delivering the fundamental points, seminars offer students the chance to ask questions and deepen, elaborate on and consolidate their knowledge.

> *The studying at university is very much an independent activity. There is nowhere near as much pressure or 'fear' instilled into you like there is at school. We have a fear at school that we may get into trouble but at uni it is just a case of – you will fail or you won't achieve what you want from the experience. It is difficult to focus at times but honesty is the best policy. Tell your tutors – they will help you!*
>
> (**Louise**, 3rd-year undergraduate)

The starting point for many seminars is a book extract or set of data which is given out in advance by the tutor. Obviously, you will get the most value from the seminar if you are able to spend time on this. If this is the format, your first task is to read and understand the arguments in the document, and your second task is to relate this to your own wider reading and perspective on the subject, so that you are able to express your opinion and support it intellectually. If you have been given more than one handout and you do not have time to read everything prior to the seminar, concentrate on one article in particular so that you are able to speak about that. You may also find it helpful to share out the articles with some colleagues and focus on one article each, with each student then providing the others with a summary of the ideas expressed. Division of labour can be very time efficient in these circumstances. Alternatively, if the literature is very difficult, you may opt to work on it with another student or write your own summary of it. You are likely to be asked to express your views, and you may find it helpful to jot these down in advance so that if your mind goes blank you can refer to your notes. Contributing to seminars becomes easier with practice, so it is important to make an attempt on each occasion. Remember that your audience is likely to be friendly and understanding, so you have nothing to lose. Indeed you have a great deal to gain as seminars offer an excellent opportunity for discussing any points you may not have understood, and for reinforcing knowledge acquired from other sources.

As with lectures, it is worth taking notes during the seminar, so that you can incorporate the points raised in any assignments or examination revision. It is also a good idea to list new terminology so that you can introduce it into your own work at a later date.

Tutorials

Tutorials are meetings between tutors and students. The tutor may see students on a one-to-one basis or in small groups. For many students, tutorials are the linchpin of the learning experience in that they offer an opportunity to draw together all that has been learned from lectures, seminars, fieldwork and private study and give the student a chance to ask questions and clarify specific points. The frequency of tutorials varies from university to university and from course to course, and in order to make the most of the precious time you have, it is wise to be well prepared. Before attending your tutorial, make a list of all the points you wish to discuss and, if possible, e-mail this to your tutor in advance so that he or she can give it some prior consideration. If you wish to talk about an assignment, try to write out a basic outline as this will make it easier for your tutor to estimate whether or not you are on the right track. Don't be afraid to voice your views and thoughts. Your tutor will not think badly of you if you have misunderstood something. Indeed, it is easier to correct a problem when one has a precise appraisal of what is involved. Do not be afraid to ask what you might consider to be 'stupid' questions. The chances are that you are not the first student to do so and your tutor will be used to explaining new concepts and correcting errors.

> *Talking to tutors can be a valuable experience. You realise they are people too and you have your area of study in common if nothing else. It helps to talk out an essay or project to clarify your ideas.*
> (**Barry**, 3rd-year undergraduate)

It is very important that you have a good working relationship with your tutor, and for this reason you should keep him or her up to date in terms of your progress and of any difficulties you encounter. If you have minor queries, these can often be addressed most efficiently in a brief exchange of e-mails, so do not be afraid to approach your tutor outside of your fixed appointments.

Fieldwork/laboratory work

Many students undertake empirical research in the form of fieldwork or laboratory work as part of their courses, either individually or in small groups. The time-scale may vary and whereas some projects can be undertaken within a day, other research may be more open-ended and take several weeks to complete. Your tutor will give you guidelines as to what is required from you, but arguably the most important piece of advice is to write down your findings as you go along. You may think that you will remember everything at a later date, but you may forget essential details or your memory may be skewed in the light of subsequent findings. It is therefore a good idea to keep some sort of a log or diary in which you can record times, dates and any observations, however trivial they may seem at the time. Ensure that these are reasonably comprehensive so that they can be easily interpreted at a later date.

Sometimes, project work is done in small groups and this can lead to difficulties if some students wish to make more effort than others. Try to allocate specific tasks to individuals early on and ensure that findings are distributed to other group members as quickly as possible. If two people are assigned to each task this will guard against the rest of the group suffering if something goes wrong or an individual does not do the work properly. If you are working as part of a group, try to arrange to meet up at regular intervals during the project. This will give everyone a chance to present feedback and discuss future plans. Working as part of a team can be rewarding and fun. Moreover, it is very good experience for the future world of paid employment.

Make sure that you are well equipped with any safety equipment and writing implements required. If you are working outside remember to take a clipboard to make note taking easier. Also, take plenty of appropriate clothing if you are likely to be outside for a long time so that you are comfortable and can deal with changes in the weather.

Some fieldwork takes place in the vacation period and if this is the case, you need as much warning as possible so that you can adapt your plans accordingly. There are often costs associated with fieldwork, and if you normally take paid employment in the vacation, this will be affected too.

Staff

You are likely to encounter a greater number of staff than you did in college or in the sixth form at school, and whereas some will get to know you well, others, particularly lecturers, may barely know you at all. In addition to lecturers and seminar tutors, you will be assigned to specific mentors, normally at least one academic tutor and one personal tutor. These are the people with whom you will have the closest contact, and to whom you can turn in case of difficulties. Your academic tutor is responsible for your intellectual development and progress and your personal tutor is responsible for advising and supporting you in your new life as an undergraduate. If possible, try to be totally honest with your tutors as this will enable them to help you when you need it. They can also liaise with each other when necessary; for example, if you have good reasons why you cannot make assignment deadlines but you would prefer not to discuss them with your academic tutor, your personal tutor can put your case without giving details, and a solution can be negotiated. If you feel you cannot talk to your personal tutor, you should approach another member of staff or the students' union for help and advice.

> The difference that I noticed the most from school to uni, and probably the most difficult, is the fact that your lecturers don't know you that well. It's not unusual for them not to know your first name, whereas at school this is virtually unknown.
> (**Harriet**, 1st-year undergraduate)

It is very important that both academic and personal problems are addressed as quickly as possible, before they become worse. Most members of staff are very amenable to addressing queries but it is often best to put your question in writing, as many lecturers and tutors do not have sufficient gaps in the timetable to see students without prior arrangement. If you are unclear about an assignment it is even more important that you ask for help early on, as it is essential that you understand what you are aiming to do before you attempt to undertake the work. Whilst you can expect to gain new insights during the course of researching the topic, you must ensure that you understand the question that has been set and that you have a definite plan for tackling it. If you are in doubt, write out a short outline and check it with the relevant tutor.

 I found that I had very little direct contact with staff and if I needed help with anything I had to make an effort to seek it out. . . . I think it can be quite daunting for new students.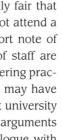
(**Henrietta**, 3rd-year undergraduate)

Members of staff will treat you as adults and therefore it is only fair that this be reciprocated. Therefore, if there is a reason why you cannot attend a class or submit a piece of work on time, you should send a short note of explanation. If kept informed of the situation, most members of staff are likely to be flexible regarding deadlines, and helpful in terms of offering practical suggestions to academic dilemmas. Whereas at school you may have been expected to keep quiet if you disagreed with your teacher, at university you will be encouraged to think for yourself and defend your own arguments and perspectives. Many lecturers and tutors welcome robust dialogue with their students! This is often reflected in the tenor of the relationship between staff and students. Many tutors are amenable to being addressed by their first names, and most encourage informal interaction during tutorials, seminars, and sometimes lectures, if points they have raised require further explanation. It may take a while to become used to speaking out to the person teaching you if you don't understand a point, or if you disagree and can support your argument, but it is important to make this transition, as interacting on an equal basis with those who have more knowledge than you is a skill that you will need when you later enter the world of work.

▶ University facilities

The library
As well as being able to access staff and attend lectures, seminars, tutorials and fieldwork activities, students also have the university facilities at their disposal. The most valuable of these is the library, and it is worth making an

effort early on to find out exactly what is on offer, as this will enable you to research topics, seek and retrieve information and locate your set texts more quickly and easily. Most university libraries offer guided tours and introductory sessions in which the procedures for borrowing books and locating specific information are explained, and it is a good idea to attend one of these. There may also be maps of the library and leaflets outlining what is available. You need to know when the library is open, how to find books and journals, how to reserve an item that is already out on loan, the duration of the loan period, which texts cannot be removed from the library, the fine system for late returns and the system for returning books outside library opening times. The library's electronic catalogue will enable you to search for texts and make reservations and it is important to familiarise yourself with this as soon as possible. You also need to know how to search the various electronic databases for information. This is particularly useful if you are looking for journal articles, and is best mastered early on so that you can reap the benefit throughout your undergraduate years. One of the key differences between school and university assignments is that the latter require wide reading. Whereas at school you may have been able to base your writing on one or two key books, at university you will be expected to cite a wide range of texts in the course of making your argument. You may be given a reading list by your tutor to get you started, or you may find that if a specific article or book is particularly relevant to your work, you are able to follow up any references within it to develop your own theme further. If you are comfortable with the electronic search facilities available, this process will be quicker and easier.

> ❛ *Studying is very different from school. You are more spoon-fed at school; you're very much on your own at uni and often don't find out vital info unless you actively go and look for it yourself.* ❜
> (**Ellie**, 3rd-year undergraduate)

As the library receives copies of all book lists to be given to students, it is likely that the key texts will be available for students to borrow, and if they are not on the shelves they can be reserved for the future. There is also the possibility of acquiring texts from elsewhere through an inter-library loan system. However, it is important not to delay once you know what you need. Inter-library loans take time, and if a lecturer recommends a book to a large number of students it will inevitably be difficult to acquire a copy. If you find that you cannot access any of the books you need, one course of action might be to try the restricted loan section. This is a small collection of the most popular books which may not be removed from the library and which may only be borrowed for a few hours at a time. Even if you normally prefer to work in your room, you may find it useful to set aside a certain period of time each week for studying in the library and taking advantage of the restricted loan collection.

Photocopying

In conjunction with this, you will need to locate the photocopying facilities within the library and ascertain whether the machines take coins or cards. As it may not be possible to obtain change once you are in the library, it is worth noting what you need in advance and making sure that you set the appropriate coins aside. Copyright laws restrict the amount you are allowed to photocopy, so check with the librarian if you are unsure. If you make photocopies, label them clearly with the author's name, the relevant book or journal title, the publisher and the publication date, as otherwise you will not be able to reference your work correctly.

Internet

You may also wish to use the Internet facilities provided by the university, particularly as lecturers and tutors increasingly refer students to specific sites for more information about certain topics. If you choose to browse the Internet for information, ensure that you are able to attribute any quotations you use correctly and use only reputable and authoritative sources of information such as university or specialist sites. A great deal of information on the Internet is misinformed or simply incorrect, so it is important to be discerning.

▶ Studying effectively

Studying at university calls for good time-management and organisational skills, plus a high level of self-discipline and motivation. In addition to attending lectures, seminars and so on, students are expected to spend considerable time reading around their subject, reviewing relevant literature, undertaking research to establish the various perspectives of an argument, organising and implementing fieldwork or project work, either individually or as part of a group, and also keeping up with assignments. These vary considerably and may take the form of written pieces, presentations or empirical work. In addition, many courses are assessed by examination, so students also need to allocate time for preparation and revision.

 I found that work wasn't put on a plate for me. Tutors and lecturers pointed me in roughly the right direction, then it was on me to

pursue study in a way that interested me. . . . There's no set things you have to learn. I've tailored my learning to what I'm interested in.

(**Nicky**, 3rd-year undergraduate)

In order to study effectively it is essential, first of all, to consider all the different demands on your time and then to construct a personal timetable that enables you to deal with the workload efficiently. Start by noting down your lectures and other university appointments and then add in any employment commitments you may have together with any regular social appointments such as club meetings. You should now have a timetable punctuated by many gaps. Bearing in mind your own personal proclivities, such as whether you work best in the morning or at night and whether you prefer to work in the library or in your room, try to allocate certain tasks to specific blocks of time, ensuring that you introduce at least one substantial session in the library per week, during which you can use the short loan collection, search the catalogues, change your books and do any on-site research required. Do not fool yourself! If you tend to get up late, do not start your study timetable early in the morning. However, if you do intend to lie in, bear in mind that there are only a limited number of hours in the day and this will count as your 'break' as well as putting pressure on the remaining time. You may also wish to schedule a regular meeting with colleagues so that, if you each decide to read and summarise one set text prior to a lecture or seminar, you have an opportunity for discussion.

The main difference between school and university is that at university if you don't do the work, no one will tell you off. Independent learning is emphasised at uni and if you don't do the work, in the end the only person who will suffer is you. It's amazing how fast you grow up. I am fairly self-motivated so I haven't really found it hard but some of my friends have struggled.

(**Louise**, 3rd-year undergraduate)

Remember that some types of work may demand more time and concentration than others; for example, you may not be able to deal with a difficult journal article after a day of lectures, whereas doing some background reading may be less onerous. It is always wise to have an alternative plan in the event of writer's block or a similar problem. If you find that you are simply unable to get your head around a particular task, you should abandon it and do something else. Talking to friends or your tutor later on may remove the block, and this way you will not have lost time overall. Plan to get the reading required for lectures and seminars done a day in advance as this gives you room for manoeuvre if you encounter unexpected difficulties. Challenge yourself but do not be unrealistic. Do not fill up your entire timetable as you will need to allow for routine tasks too, such as shopping, cooking and doing the laundry. Make sure that you allow time for breaks and do not be tempted to work through them. You will feel more refreshed if you stop and have a coffee, glance at the newspaper or chat to a flatmate. Also, try to ensure that if you have a particularly hard day you arrange some sort of social reward for yourself at the end of it, so that you have something to which you can look forward. Once you have devised a timetable that works for you, it becomes a matter of self-discipline to stick to it. Temptations and distractions will inevitably arise, but if you can redirect them to your next free period, you are likely to achieve your study goals without missing out on social opportunities.

 I always find it difficult to work at home so . . . get out of the house and work where there are no distractions.
(**Charlie**, 3rd-year undergraduate)

In addition to planning your personal timetable, you need to ensure that you have an efficient filing system and that all your notes are comprehensive, including full details of any references you may later wish to cite. Do not try to economise on stationery by keeping everything in one or two files. Keep notes, photocopies and handouts relating to each topic in a separate folder, preferably colour coded, and label them clearly. You may also find it helpful to acquire an academic diary (which runs from September through to the end of the following year) in order to keep track of your deadlines, plus a notebook in which you can list all the work that you currently need to tackle. 'Post-it' notes are invaluable too, as reminders of specific outstanding tasks.

▶ Forms of assessment

Some of the work you do at university will be assessed. You may be asked to submit a piece of written work, undertake a research project either alone or with colleagues, give a presentation or sit an examination. As with other aspects of undergraduate study, there are ways of maximising your chances of success, and these are outlined briefly below. Students who require more detailed information may wish to consult a specialist publication such as *The Study Skills Handbook*.[47]

Writing an essay

The main difference between writing an essay in college or the sixth form at school and writing at university is that the latter calls not only for an account of related literature and views but also for an analysis of it. You will be expected to make an argument and support your perspective with evidence. Therefore, there are two distinct stages to an essay assignment: research and writing.

It is wise not to begin writing until you have a comprehensive understanding of the topic in question and a firm idea of your own stance in relation to it. In order to achieve this you need to read around the subject. Start with any relevant lecture and seminar notes and then explore further. You can often find useful additional sources for information by reading through the footnotes and references in your primary text. Searching the library catalogue can often yield results too, as can looking on the Internet. However, as mentioned previously, it is important to be wary of information found on the Internet as the source may not be authoritative, and the content may be inaccurate or misleading. Keep notes on anything relevant that you read and may wish to include and photocopy articles that are of particular importance. Make up a folder of background research before you begin to write and remember to draw on it throughout your essay as you will get credit for wide reading and research.

> ❛ On my course all my essays are due in the same week at the end of each semester. I have had to learn ways of motivating myself to start working weeks before the deadlines in order to get everything finished on time. Investing in a diary and planning work from the start is the most important thing to do. ❜
>
> (**Cassie**, 3rd-year undergraduate)

If you cite or quote from someone else's work, you must acknowledge this in your referencing. Moreover, at university level, it is not sufficient merely to mention others' views on the topic: you should then analyse any claims made and support your opinion with evidence from other research findings or academic observations. It does not matter whether or not you agree with your tutor's views, as long as you can support your own argument intellectually. Plagiarism – copying from others without due acknowledgment – has always been a problem, but it has become more widespread with the development of the Internet, and should be avoided at all costs. Universities tend to monitor cheat sites regularly and most have invested in sophisticated software to detect plagiarism. If caught, the consequences for the student are very serious, and can include expulsion.

> ❛ *The change [between studying at school and at university] is huge, especially doing an arts degree where very little is compulsory. Basically a title is set with a reading list and then it's up to me to do the work. It was difficult to adapt at first and I found myself being really lazy. One of the biggest transitions was learning self-discipline.* ❜
>
> (**Annabel**, 3rd-year undergraduate)

A common problem when writing an essay is to finish the research and then feel unable to start writing. Anxiety about the approaching deadline may then compound the situation. If this happens to you, you could try one or more of the following suggestions:

▶ Write an outline plan and then spend time making it more and more detailed, noting where you will bring in your reading and references.

▶ Draw a 'mind map' of all the points you wish to include and then try to arrange them in a logical order.

▶ Brainstorm with a colleague.

▶ If the introduction is causing you problems, leave it until later and start with a section you feel secure about.

▶ Make a list of the points you wish to include, or lists for and against the argument expressed in the question.

▶ Summarise what you wish to say in a single paragraph and then expand on it.

▶ Write a list of headings and subheadings to be included.

▶ Promise yourself a reward if you write a specific amount by a certain time.

▶ Remember that this is only a draft so write down what comes to mind with a view to honing it later.

▶ If you are easily distracted whilst in your room, go to the library to write your essay.

It is far easier to amend a draft than to write from scratch, so try to get your thoughts down in writing as soon as you can. Then you can perfect your choice of words and expressions and run a spelling and grammar check. If you read your essay aloud you will soon notice if the language is convoluted or confused. Pay particular attention to your introduction and conclusion and make sure that both are clear. Once you are happy with your essay, set it aside for a day and then reread it before printing it out and handing it in. Take note of any feedback which may also apply to your future work.

Writing up fieldwork/lab notes

As I have outlined earlier in this chapter, the key piece of advice for students who are required to submit a report on field research or laboratory work is to take comprehensive notes at the time, so that there is a plentiful supply of data when the time comes to write up the report.

You will be given guidelines on how to set out your work and what details to include. Normally, these will include the hypothesis to be tested, an introduction (to include the location for the research, the apparatus, materials and participants if relevant), the method, observations, findings and conclusions. You may be expected to include notes on whether or not your findings were expected, and to comment on the limitations of your particular study/experiment/survey. The language and style should be scientific in nature and you may wish to include charts and graphs to display your data. Sometimes an abstract is required. This is a succinct summary of the report which is presented immediately after the title. It is a good idea to write the abstract after you have completed writing the report.

Giving a presentation

If you are required to give a presentation, it is important to establish the length of the time slot and the intended purpose. If, for example, you have a 15-minute period in which to present your research findings you may wish to devote five minutes to set the scene, three minutes to comment on relevant literature and publications, and the rest of the time to a structured account of your research. This could include what you set out to achieve, your method, your findings, and your interpretation of the results.

Spoken accounts are very different from written accounts and the best way to make sure that the tenor of your talk is appropriate is to practise it aloud several times beforehand. This will also verify whether it is of the correct length. You should speak slowly and clearly, and, whilst it is perfectly acceptable to refer to notes, you should not simply read out your presentation. You should begin with some clear introductory sentences, and then give an idea of the structure of your talk so that your audience knows what to expect. If you can use PowerPoint or transparencies this is likely to bring your presentation to life, and make it more interesting for those listening. Ensure that you have a strong closing sentence and be prepared to answer questions.

Sitting an examination

Examinations can be very nerve-wracking, and the best antidote to this is good long-term preparation. Long before the examination, you are likely to have devised a strategy for keeping comprehensive lecture and seminar notes that relate to the topic concerned, and filing them in an organised manner. Similarly, you will have labelled all relevant photocopies and made notes on recommended books and articles. If this is the case it is now a matter of reading through all your notes, writing short summaries or highlighting key aspects, and learning the salient points by heart. You can also increase your chances of doing well by looking at past examination papers and thinking about how you would answer the questions. Make sure you eat healthily and take frequent breaks during revision periods, and try to quell any nerves by talking to friends, or, failing that, by reminding yourself that you are well prepared. Try to get plenty of rest the night before and ensure that you arrive in good time for the exam and that you have everything you require in terms of stationery and equipment. If you are not sure of the location, check out where it is in the preceding days.

When you turn over the examination paper, read the instructions carefully and take a few moments to decide which questions to answer and to plan how you intend to allocate the time allowed. You may wish to make notes or a brief outline. Reread the question from time to time to ensure that you have taken note of what is required and that the content of your answer is absolutely relevant to the question asked. If you begin to run out of time, summarise the rest of your argument in a paragraph and move on to the next question. Try to stay positive and focused, and direct all your energy to the job in hand. Afterwards, refrain from lengthy postmortems with your colleagues as these can be demoralising. Instead, allow yourself some sort of celebration, and move on to consolidate your preparation for the next exam.

▶ Dealing with problems

Unsurprisingly, problems often do arise as students try to come to terms with the demands of a new study regime in an unfamiliar environment. It can take a while to understand what is expected and to organise one's time efficiently to ensure that the work gets done. Some students are initially overwhelmed by the large numbers in attendance at lectures and the many booklists; others are daunted if the texts they need are not available and they cannot see how to proceed with an assignment. These feelings can be compounded by the demands of independent student life, particularly if that too presents new challenges. It is important to realise that nearly everybody needs a settling-in period and time to get used to a new system. So, if you are feeling worried or unsure about your work, try not to worry. Many problems tend to resolve themselves over the first few weeks.

If you can identify your specific concerns, you are well on the way to sorting them out. Many problems relate specifically to issues of inappropriate time management or lack of organisation. If this is the case, look at your timetable and try to restructure it so that you have sufficient time for private study, library work and so on, as well as your lectures and seminars. Some students throw themselves into student life so wholeheartedly when they first arrive at university that there is insufficient time left for studying and the tasks accumulate until the workload seems insurmountable. If this happens, do not despair, but instead try to break down your commitments into manageable sections, and tackle them methodically. In many cases, with a slightly different mind-set and a little reorganisation you will be able to sort out your problems and devise a timetable and strategy that will avoid future difficulties.

However, if you cannot see what to do for the best, it is essential that you seek advice as soon as possible. Talk to your academic tutor and your personal tutor, as they are best placed to help you. They will, for example, be able to help you devise a plan for catching up on missed work or for filling in gaps in your knowledge. Keep a note of all your areas of concern and track whether or not you feel you are making progress. You may find it helpful to talk to other students and listen to their experiences too.

> In my experience some students find it difficult to adapt to the culture of independent study required at university. Motivating themselves to work when they are not being frequently monitored by lecturers is a challenge. This coupled with the distractions of a new city, new friends and a busy social life means that students often take the first term properly to settle into their studies.
>
> (**Beatrice**, tutor)

It is also very common for students in the first few weeks to question whether they have made the right choice of course, or even if university is right for them. If you have such thoughts you should discuss the matter with your tutor as soon as possible – sometimes a slight change in modules can make all the difference. You may also wish to speak to the student counsellor if you are unhappy, as your problems may actually be related to leaving home rather than your course itself. Try to be patient and accept that it does take time to settle in to university life. However, if you remain fairly sure that you would be happier studying another subject or changing universities, it is sensible to check out your options. Try to establish the root of the problem so that you can avoid it if you do make changes; for example, identify whether it is the subject itself that is causing you concern, or the method of assessment, or something to do with the university such as its size or location.

Although it is better to transfer earlier rather than later, it is also important to give yourself time to ensure that you really do wish to change. Sharing your thoughts with your tutor should help you to approach the situation analytically and not simply let your emotions take over. While you are in this transitional phase you can make enquiries about other options such as the possibility of transferring courses, and the logistics involved. Once you have made your final decision, the next course of action will become apparent.

▶ Summary

This chapter has given an insight into studying at university, focusing particularly on how to derive the maximum value from lectures, seminars, supervised fieldwork and tutorials. It has emphasised the need for self-motivation and the importance of making good use of staff expertise and university facilities such as the library. It has offered guidelines on effective study techniques and has suggested how to tackle problems.

▶ More Feedback . . .

Students are often reluctant to avail themselves of help offered by tutors with assignments. For example, the tutor might be willing to look at a plan or a draft version of an essay in progress, but students frequently won't submit their plan or draft for comment. I suspect the reason is often that students do all the work at the last minute but it can also be that students want to avoid receiving criticism of their work if they think that they perform badly academically. They would rather give the work in at the deadline and try to forget about it until it is marked and returned, than to learn its weaknesses in time to improve it. Of course, another reason for failing to take up offers of help can also be laziness or lack of motivation: it's less work to just do the thing once no matter how much the assignment could have been improved following some comments from the tutor. It's such a pity because tutors who offer to see students' work in progress genuinely want to help students to improve their work and they are usually sensitive to the students' feelings about their work.

(**Jo**, tutor)

8 Health, Safety and Security

This chapter will give advice on health, safety and security issues. In particular, it will:

- look at what you should do if you become ill at university
- identify where to get help, information or advice on health-related issues including contraception and other sexual matters, smoking, alcohol and drugs
- provide information on healthy eating and food hygiene
- outline the steps you can take to enhance your personal safety and safeguard your possessions

▶ Taking control of your physical well-being

Most students living at home take their health and well-being for granted. For many, the family structure means that if they are ill, they can easily make an appointment with their GP or ask for a home visit, and also call upon parents and siblings for advice and help with medication and nursing care. Often, it is a parent who will take responsibility for the nutritional requirements of the family and, similarly, parents may also assist with their children's safety and security arrangements, by ensuring that adequate plans are in place or by providing a parental taxi service. So, for many students, going to university may mean taking charge of their personal well-being for the first time.

> ❛ I never really took care of my physical well-being at home because my mother was always the one interested in my health. Once I arrived at university I found myself having to choose what food to cook and eat. I realised how bad some food can be for your health and I started buying food exclusively from the

organics section to improve my diet. I also began to take multi-vitamins and vitamin C every morning to give me extra strength as I immediately caught the freshers' flu. Fortunately with all the vitamins and the organic food I really feel that I am healthy and this helps me enjoy my student life even more.

(**Amy**, 1st-year undergraduate)

▶ **Basics**

When you first go to university it is essential that you register with a GP. This will mean that if you subsequently become ill you will be able to make an appointment at the surgery, or, if you are too ill to attend, you will be able to arrange a home visit. A recent NUS survey on healthcare involving over 1500 respondents revealed that one in ten students was not registered with a doctor at all, and one in seven students did not seek medical help when the need arose. Of those who did not register, most cited either lack of time or lack of knowledge about how to access local health services as the key problems.[48] However, it is actually very easy to register with a GP. Most universities either have their own doctors, or can supply students with a list of local doctors. Failing that, NHS Direct (telephone number 0845 46 47; website www.nhsdirect.nhs.uk), can provide details of GPs in the local area for students in England and Wales. Students in Scotland should contact NHS 24 (telephone number 0845 4 24 24 24). Each practice has its own procedures for new patients, but most involve filling in a form at the surgery. These telephone advice lines can also supply information on registering with an NHS dentist or locating a late-night pharmacy in a particular area. It is preferable to register not only with a GP but also with a dentist and an optician, and to be aware of where to ask for help and further information if necessary.

If you have concerns about your health but are not sure whether or not you should see a doctor, NHS Direct or NHS 24 (numbers above) can also help with medical enquiries, since their remit is to provide a 24-hour confidential helpline focusing on all health issues and concerns. They provide a comprehensive service ranging from advice and information about local support or self-help organisations and health policy to providing medically trained staff to discuss your individual symptoms and advise on the best course of action. If you are at all worried, these are useful numbers to have. Alternatively, you may want to look up your symptoms on the Internet without discussing them with anyone. Obviously, this opens up the possibility of inadvertently ignoring serious symptoms or focusing too heavily on minor ones, but if you do take this course of action, there are various sites that can help you, including www.nusonline.co.uk. However, it is wise to seek trained medical advice if you feel unwell, especially as some diseases require prompt action. It is better to be safe than sorry, especially with regard to outbreaks of potentially serious diseases such as meningitis and mumps amongst students.

> *I think the most important thing to do when joining university is to join sports societies to meet like-minded people. The university surfing club for me has allowed me to stay fit and meet a wealth of people. As far as doctors go, it's important to join the Health Service immediately as you never know what may happen. I for one didn't and managed to rather spectacularly fracture my skull kayaking. Trying to arrange check-up appointments afterwards was more than hard work as the processing time for doctor application forms can't seem to be hurried.*
> (**Richard**, 3rd-year undergraduate)

It is also sensible to keep some basic medication in your room, such as over-the-counter medicine to deal with flu and colds, stomach upsets, headaches and hangovers. If you are suddenly taken ill, and there is nobody at hand to help, this is not the best time to have to go out in search of a pharmacy, especially if the problem occurs in the night. Many new undergraduates succumb to 'freshers' flu' in the first few weeks, as germs spread quickly when groups of infected people are in close proximity with others, especially when many of those concerned have weakened immune systems due to an over-demanding lifestyle with insufficient food and rest and a tendency to burn the candle at both ends. A sensible move would be to equip yourself with the appropriate medication so that if you do become ill, you can look after yourself.

> *Keeping healthy is a problem but an orange a day is a start. There are so many bugs around and the endless lack of sleep lowers your resistance. If you have to work on a presentation all night, the only answer is a six-pack of caffeine drinks!*
> (**Sara**, 3rd-year undergraduate)

Students in full-time education are entitled to free medical treatment including free eye tests until their eighteenth birthday and an exemption from prescription charges together with free dental treatment until their nineteenth birthday. After that, they will be asked to pay a charge. However, many students on a low income, irrespective of nationality, can apply for financial help with health costs under the NHS Low Income Scheme.

Services covered include dental treatment, prescription fees and opticians' costs. Applicants need to complete an HC1 form which is available from a number of sources including, (for students in England, Scotland and Wales) hospitals, some pharmacies, GP surgeries, opticians and dentists, the Department of Health Publication Line (telephone 08701 555 455, e-mail dh@prolog.uk.com), or the Prescription Pricing Authority (telephone helpline 0845 8501166, website www.ppa.org.uk). Students in Northern Ireland should contact their local health authority for the form. More detailed information about the scheme is available from the above-mentioned sources in the HC11 information booklet, which accompanies the HC1 application form. Charges do vary in England, Scotland, Wales and Northern Ireland, for example, under-25s in Wales receive most health benefits free, so it is important to identify the arrangements that apply to your particular situation.

> *Going to the gym a few times a week really helped to relieve stress and make sure I was doing some exercise. That was a good thing as at school I used to play hockey in the team and I missed not having a sport to play when I got here.*
> (**Rakesh**, 3rd-year undergraduate)

▶ Specific information and advice

In addition to the helpline numbers relating to general queries about health concerns, it is useful to know how to obtain further information and advice on specific issues relating to your health and well-being, such as sexual health, contraception, alcohol, drugs and smoking. Information is usually available from your students' union or GP, but you may also find it convenient to check out key national helplines and specialist organisations.

Alcohol
There is no denying that alcohol plays a large part in university social life. If kept under control, drinking is enjoyable and can add to a social event. The key to success is to stay in control of your alcohol intake and not let it take control of you. This is more difficult than it sounds in an environment in which the peer pressure to drink may be intense, the opportunities to drink more frequent, and a common misconception may be that alcohol does not cause serious problems. It is probably because alcohol is so widely accepted in contemporary society that many people simply do not regard it as a problem. However, to put this in perspective, approximately half the number of adults admitted to hospital with head injuries are drunk, and about the

same percentage of pedestrians aged 16–60 who are killed in road accidents have alcohol about the drink-drive limit in their bloodstream.[49] Most people are aware of the Government directives on how much alcohol can be drunk safely and what is considered to be harmful. If you want to check the facts on alcohol, you can do so by contacting Alcohol Concern (telephone 0207 928 7377 or website www.alcoholconcern.org.uk). You can also order copies of a range of leaflets on alcohol consumption produced by the Department of Health by telephoning the NHS Responseline on 08701 555 455. If you are worried about your own or someone else's drinking, you can get confidential information, advice and support from Drinkline on 0800 917 8282.

> Drink but don't drink loads. I got alcohol poisoning and was very unwell.
>
> (**Olivia**, 3rd-year undergraduate)

It is very important that you don't drink more than you want to, and you can achieve this by setting yourself a limit and sticking to it, alternating non-alcoholic drinks with alcoholic ones, or switching to non-alcoholic drinks when you have had enough, refusing drinks if you don't want any more, drinking slowly, and not getting involved with rounds as they are likely to mean drinking more than you intend. There are many good reasons for enjoying drinking alcohol but stopping before you get completely drunk. If you are drunk, as well as being more likely to be sick within a few hours and hungover the next day, you are also more likely to do something you may later regret. However, if you control your alcohol intake you are likely to look and feel better, enjoy better health, make your money go further, get home safely and get up without problems the next day.

> I keep healthy by doing sport. There are loads of opportunities and you can get really fit without realising. I have dropped a dress size in two months and I'm eating all the same rubbish I used to. One way of keeping healthy is choosing a campus university because the combination of no money and nothing to do (except work and the dreaded and infamous union), means you'll walk any distance in search of a decent night out or some shops.
>
> (**Helen**, 2nd-year undergraduate)

Smoking

The NHS Smoking Helpline notes that although smoking is currently the largest single cause of death in the UK, if you stop before you reach middle age you will avoid more than 90 per cent of the health risks associated with smoking.[50] The first step if you want to stop or if you require further information is to call the helpline on 0800 169 0 169 or visit the website, www.givingupsmoking.co.uk. Advisers are on hand to listen to your questions and concerns and offer advice and support. They can also put you in touch with groups in your area, and send you relevant literature, such as the Department of Health booklet *Giving up for Life*. Other organisations that can offer help include ASH (Action on Smoking and Health), telephone 020 7739 5902, website www.ash.org.uk, and Quit, telephone 0800 00 22 00, website www.quit.org.uk.

Drugs

The adverse effects of drugs are frequently reported in the national press and include a range of health problems, impaired judgement, addiction and anti-social behaviour. Using certain drugs can also have fatal consequences. Unsurprisingly, many people prefer to steer well clear of the drugs scene. However, drug use is part of contemporary life and if you are involved in drugs, or you know someone who is, it is sensible to have access to as much information as possible in order to make informed choices. If you need information or advice about drugs, you can telephone the National Drugs Helpline ('talk to Frank') 0800 77 66 00. The Textphone number for deaf callers is 0800 917 8765. Alternatively you can check out the website www.talk-tofrank.com. 'Frank' offers confidential advice on a number of drug-related issues, such as the effects and risks of various drugs, how the law classifies drugs into one of three categories – A, B, and C; (A being the most harmful) – and what the legal implications are for possession. Frank gives advice on tackling peer pressure, and can also post out free leaflets on drug-related concerns. If you type in your town or postcode on the website, Frank can deliver a list of organisations offering support and practical help in your area. Scotland has a separate drugs line called Know the Score, which can be reached by telephone (0800 587 5789) or website www.knowthescore.info.

Sexual health

There are a number of organisations dedicated to offering advice and support on a wide range of sexual issues. As many organisations cover more than one aspect, the information in this section is intended primarily as a starting point for students. In addition to the contacts given, you may of course seek advice from your GP or from NHS Direct (telephone 0845 46 47; website www.nhsdirect.nhs.uk).

For advice and information on contraception, contact Brook (telephone 0800 0185 023 or website www.brook.org.uk). Brook provides confidential advice on sexual health and free contraception for young people under the age of 25. The Family Planning Association (helpline in the UK 0845 310 1334, in Scotland 0141 576 5088, in Belfast 028 90 325 488, in Derry 028 71 260 016, or website www.fpa.org.uk) also offers advice on a range of sexual health issues and if you phone the helpline you can request details of your nearest family planning clinic which will enable you to obtain free contraception.

These organisations also offer advice on pregnancy and will be able to direct you if you wish to discuss your options with a counsellor. If you call either the Brook or the FPA helpline, an adviser will be able to let you know where to go to get the 'morning after' pill free of charge. Abortions are free through the NHS and require a referral from two doctors. However, you can also obtain a private abortion for a fee from either the British Pregnancy Advisory Service (telephone in UK 08457 30 40 30, from Ireland 44 121 450 7700 or website www.bpas.org) or Marie Stopes Clinics (telephone 0845 300 80 90 or website www.mariestopes.org.uk). The Marie Stopes helpline is open 24 hours a day, 7 days a week, so if you need someone to talk to outside of office hours, that is a good place to start.

If you require information about sexual health, you can get free, confidential advice from the Sexual Health Line on 0800 567 123 (www.playingsafely.co.uk). Sexual Health Wales (0845 604 8484) is available for young people in Wales. If you require information about HIV or you would like to talk to someone in confidence, call the Terence Higgins Trust helpline on 0845 1221 200 (website www.tht.org.uk). The Terence Higgins Trust is committed to enabling callers to make an informed choice about sexual matters and HIV. If you would like detailed information about other sexually transmitted infections (STIs), such as chlamydia, gonorrhoea, syphilis, genital herpes or genital warts, you can either phone the Sexual Health Line or the Family Planning Association (helpline in UK 0845 310 1334, in Scotland 0141 576 5088, in Belfast 028 90 325 488, in Derry 028 71 260 016, or website www.fpa.org.uk) or access the relevant fact-sheets on the Health Protection Agency's website www.hpa.org.uk/infections. Look under 'topics a–z' and then 'HIV and sexually transmitted infections'. The site includes general information, publications and contact numbers together with information on how to reduce the risk of contacting these infections considerably by using condoms appropriately and consistently. If you do wish to seek medical advice, you can either see your GP or refer yourself to a free and completely confidential GUM (genitorurinary medicine) or STD (sexually transmitted diseases) clinic. The Sexual Health Line can advise you about clinics in your area.

Rape crisis groups exist across the UK and Ireland, and if you need the contact number of your local centre, this can be accessed via www.

rapecrisis.org.uk. This site also provides information on the myths surrounding rape, the court process, and relevant facts and figures. The Roofie Foundation (telephone 0800 783 2980 or website www.roofie.com) is a one-stop shop and advisory centre for victims of drug-related rape and sexual abuse.

 At the union, rape alarms were given out which I thought was a really good thing.

(**Rakesh**, 3rd-year undergraduate)

Emotional support

The Samaritans can be reached on 08457 909090 (Republic of Ireland 1850 60 90 90). They offer a 24-hour confidential helpline for anyone in crisis. If you have a problem that you feel you can't deal with, and you need to talk to someone, phone the Samaritans who are ready to listen and discuss anything.

If you are troubled by concerns about your sexual orientation and you need support, you are likely to find that your students' union can help. Universities usually have a gay and lesbian society together with a specific officer responsible for offering advice, information and support to gay students. Alternatively, you may wish to call the London Lesbian and Gay Switchboard on 020 7837 7324 or to look at their listings on www.queery.org.uk. If you are thinking of coming out and need time to reflect before talking to anyone about it, you may find it helpful to look at www.stonewall.org.uk under 'information' and 'coming out' for a sympathetic and comprehensive view. Stonewall is a campaigning organisation which lobbies for gay equality to be on the mainstream political agenda, and the information section also includes a list of support services by area.

Other

If your problem or circumstances have not been covered above, you may wish to look up www.helplines.org.uk and see if there is a specific organisation listed there that can help you.

▶ Keeping healthy

The best way to achieve a healthy lifestyle is to try to get a reasonable amount of exercise, sufficient sleep, an appropriate ratio between work and leisure, regular meals and a balanced diet.

 Join the gym, go jogging, sleep well, don't burn the candle at both ends all the time, learn to cook properly.

(**Charlie**, 3rd-year undergraduate)

Healthy eating

It is very important that you give some thought to your diet, as a healthy and varied diet is essential for your overall well-being. Try to eat a variety of different foods and, each day, try to include one or two items from each of the following categories in your diet: fruit and vegetables; milk and dairy products; meat, fish and alternatives; bread, cereals or potatoes. In order to remain healthy it is best to maintain a good balance between carbohydrate, fat and protein and choosing daily from the options listed above will help to ensure this. The British Nutrition Foundation (BNF) recommends eating a variety of foods in sufficient quantity to maintain a healthy weight, including ample fruit, vegetables and foods rich in starch and fibre, avoiding too many foods heavy in fat, avoiding too many sugary foods and drinks and limiting salt and alcohol intake as per government guidelines. The BNF offers many suggestions for healthy eating on its website (www.nutrition.org.uk) and, in addition, has leaflets on various specific aspects of nutrition which can be ordered via the website.

> *The uni fruit man is a fantastic way of getting cheap fresh fruit and veg. My friends say he may go out of business when I graduate. The supermarket's reduced section is especially full just before it shuts – buy lots of stuff and freeze it!*
> (**Steph**, 3rd-year undergraduate)

You may find that for the first time you are responsible for your own diet, and you may also find that due to the new demands of student life, you may inadvertently miss meals or forget to buy food in good time. Do not try to economise by cutting out meals as this will make you ill. Instead, include inexpensive but healthy foods in your diet such as fruit, vegetables, bread, pasta and sauce. If possible, try to plan your menus so that you can do all your shopping in one go. You will undoubtedly need snacks during the day, particularly if you are working in your room. Try to avoid consuming vast amounts of biscuits – snacking on fruit or raw vegetables is far healthier. The Government's 'five a day' campaign, launched in 2003, extolled the benefits of five portions of fruit or vegetables every day (see www.dh.gov.uk). Fruit is easy to store and keeps for a reasonable time. As such it is an excellent snack food for students. You may also find it helpful to keep a packet of breakfast cereal and some long-life milk in your room (if you don't have access to a fridge) in case of emergencies. (See also Chapter 3 for what to keep in your store cupboard if you are self-catering.)

A can of beans equals one portion of your fruit and veg recommended daily amount, and goes excellently with lightly toasted brown bread.

(**William**, 3rd-year undergraduate)

Food hygiene

The National Union of Students notes that an estimated one in ten people in the UK suffer from illnesses that are food related.[51] For this reason, it is very important to be aware of good practices with regard to food hygiene, and to follow them. Whilst preparing food it is essential to prevent germs spreading and cross-contamination occurring. The main safeguards against this are to wash your hands with soap and warm water and dry them thoroughly before touching food, after touching raw meat, and at other obviously appropriate times, such as if you use the toilet or stroke a pet. You should also wash the kitchen surfaces and utensils, particularly chopping boards and knives, before starting to prepare food and after any interaction with raw meat, fish and poultry. To prevent bacteria from spreading, remember to keep raw meat away from other food, both during preparation and also when it is stored in the fridge. In this instance it should be covered and placed on the bottom shelf so that it cannot drip on to other food. After use, all utensils should be washed in hot water and washing-up liquid and left to drain, as tea towels can be haven for bacteria. You may prefer to use disposable kitchen roll to clean work surfaces as cloths harbour germs and students often do not have the facilities to wash them sufficiently frequently. Finally, try to keep the fridge and cupboards as clean as possible, and empty the rubbish regularly.

 I'm not overly healthy but I try to eat vegetables and buy healthy-living meals.

(**Samantha**, 2nd-year undergraduate)

If you are cooking meat, ensure that it is hot in the middle and there is no pink meat left. Do not be tempted to eat food that has passed its sell-by date, and keep food in the fridge, if appropriate, until just before you intend to cook it, to ensure that it remains in good condition. If you reheat food it is important to ensure that it is very hot all the way through because if it is not, harmful bacteria in it may make you ill. If in doubt, heat it for a bit longer. Many prepared dishes cannot be reheated twice. Read the instructions carefully and don't take chances. If you cook a dish from scratch and don't eat it all at the first sitting, cool the rest quickly and store it in the fridge. Leftovers should be consumed as soon as possible, and definitely within 48 hours.

If you need further information about healthy eating and food hygiene, this can be obtained from the Food Standards Agency (www.eatwell.gov.uk).

► Personal safety

It's very important to go out and socialise, especially when you first arrive at university and want to meet new people, and you will soon find that there are ample opportunities for this. However, whereas at home you probably went out with an established group of friends to familiar places, at first everything at university will be new. You may not know the area very well, or be in a position to make plans for going out with others. It is therefore well worth thinking in advance about how to keep safe, especially if you are likely to be returning to your room alone and late at night.

> *An important thing that I found to be extremely useful before I started at uni was to visit the area a few times before I started. I really think that having an idea of where you are and how to get back to your halls from anywhere in campus is an integral part of being safe at uni. The first year of uni is a time for students to experiment with new things, from drink to new courses and friends. My advice is, enjoy it . . . but be safe.*
>
> (**Chloe**, 3rd-year undergraduate)

It is always best to travel with other people, on the basis that there is safety in numbers. However, if this is not possible, think ahead about how you will get home, and if possible, let someone else know your plans. Look up the late bus times and put the telephone numbers of one or two reputable taxi companies in your mobile phone, in case of emergencies. Don't ever get into an unmarked taxi. If you are walking, try to choose well-lit, busy routes and do not be tempted to take short cuts. Be aware of those around you and if you think that you are being followed, go to a public place and call the police. If you are carrying a bag, turn the fastener in towards your body and wear the strap across your shoulder and body. In any case, keep your keys and a small amount of money in a separate pocket so that if you do lose your bag you still have the resources to get home safely. Do not walk down the road talking on your mobile phone. Try to make any calls before you set off and keep your phone out of sight. You may wish to carry a personal alarm, and if so, you should keep it in your hand ready for use. It is very important to look positive and in control, so if you do need to check where you are on a map, do so discreetly before you set off and then walk briskly and confidently. If you have drunk more than you intended, consider taking a taxi home, especially if you don't know the area well.

 Always take taxis after dark – organise life so that you don't need to be walking anywhere in the dark.
(**Sam**, 3rd-year undergraduate)

There has been a great deal of coverage in the press about date rape, in which drinks are spiked with drugs such as rohypnol or methodone, resulting in a loss of control and memory. Victims of date rape have reported large gaps in memory or recollections of sexual encounters to which they would never willingly have consented. You can find out more information about this from the Roofie Foundation's website on www.roofie.com. This organisation offers advice and support to victims of drug-related rape and also has a helpline on 0800 783 2980. The best guard against drug rape is to make sure that you never leave your drink unattended, that you don't accept drinks from people you don't trust, and that you watch as your drinks are served. If you feel at all strange you should tell someone immediately, as most clubs have emergency rooms and someone who can help. If you are with a friend, ask them to take you home. If someone you are with starts to behave strangely, or seems compliant when a person or persons they do not know suggests they leave together, you should check that there is nothing amiss. Students who are in groups and who are looking out for one another are best placed to avoid this sort of problem, particularly if they have prearranged plans to travel home together.

Being safe is quite important. Once it's dark I will avoid walking places on my own and always get the bus home from uni even though it is not very direct and takes a lot longer than walking. It ensures I stay safe and drops me near my house. Staying to well-lit and fairly busy areas is important. Also silly things like making sure the door is locked.
(**Marina**, 2nd-year undergraduate)

If, when you are out, you do encounter problems, such as a confrontation or altercation, try to avoid getting involved. Once you are safely out of the area you can then call the police if you think they should intervene. Stay aware of your environment at all times and do not be afraid to shout if someone approaches you. If, despite all your precautions, you are mugged, you should hand over your bag or wallet rather than fighting to keep it. These items can always be replaced. If you are the victim of a mugging, notify the police and the university, and if you need to talk through what has happened with someone sympathetic, contact the university counselling service or www.victimsupport.org.uk (helpline 0845 30 30 900).

> ❛ When I first came to uni, I thought everyone would be quite normal, but as a general rule I would still say 'don't talk to strangers', especially when drunk! People can be just as dodgy when they're students! Also, the importance of being able to drink copious amounts of alcohol truly becomes clear!   ❜
>
> (**Emma**, 3rd-year undergraduate)

In terms of your personal safety at your place of residence, it is important that anywhere you rent achieves the safety standards outlined in Chapter 6. However, you also need to ensure that you know how to turn off the gas, electricity and water supplies if necessary. If your gas cooker leaks gas, or you smell gas at all, you need to turn off the supply, open the windows, and immediately telephone Transco's 24-hour emergency line on 0800 111999. Gas is highly flammable, so, as well as avoiding the use of matches, it is also important not to turn any lights on or use any electrical appliances at all.

You may also wish to club together with your flatmates and purchase a carbon monoxide detector, as this will warn you of faulty appliances leaking carbon monoxide, which has no smell, but which can cause drowsiness, sickness, and, eventually, can be fatal. If you need any further information about policy or landlords' duties with regard to gas appliances, this can be obtained from the Health and Safety Executive's Gas Safety Action Line on 0800 300 363.

► Safeguarding possessions

Home Office statistics indicate that each year one in three students at university will be the victim of a crime.[52] In many cases students will lose personal possessions as a result of burglary and for this reason it is very important to have adequate insurance in place, preferably before arriving at university. In some cases students are covered by their parents' home insurance, but if not, specialist firms such as Endsleigh (www.endsleigh.co.uk or freephone 0800 028 3571) offer packages that are tailor-made for students, as do certain banks such as HSBC and NatWest. For those who feel they simply cannot afford general insurance it is still worth looking into the cost of covering major items such as laptop computers and televisions.

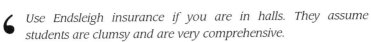

> *Use Endsleigh insurance if you are in halls. They assume students are clumsy and are very comprehensive.*
>
> (**Guy**, 3rd-year undergraduate)

The key to safeguarding your possessions is a combination of vigilance and good practice. Burglars and muggers are likely to go for the easy option, so if you take simple precautions you will make life significantly more difficult for them and perhaps deter them from targeting you and your possessions. These may include the following:

> *I used to hear a lot of horror stories about xxx because it's such a big city. But the college has done as much as it can to keep us safe. The halls of residence – you have to swipe in with your swipe cards so only students can get in. I know some of my friends have had trouble with pickpockets but so far, touch wood, I've been pretty lucky.*
>
> (**Azura**, 3rd-year undergraduate)

- ▶ Ensure that you have good locks, preferably deadlocks, on your door and windows.
- ▶ Always lock your door when you are not in the room, even if you are just going to be away for half an hour.
- ▶ Do not let strangers in. This may seem obvious, but it is very easy to be followed in through the main door of a hall of residence by someone who has no business there, or to feel pressurised to admit a 'friend' of a flatmate if the latter is not at home.
- ▶ Shut and lock your windows before you go out.
- ▶ Make sure that no valuables are visible through the window. Put everything away, and ensure that car keys do not identify your car easily and are kept out of sight. Draw the curtains if appropriate. You may wish to invest in a lockable trunk to go under your bed. Whilst this could still be stolen, it is cumbersome and may make a burglar think twice. You could store all your personal effects such as your passport and credit cards in it if you do not have a lockable drawer.
- ▶ Invest in a timer light to disguise when you are in and out, or leave a light on.
- ▶ Do not advertise your absence, for example with notes for friends on your door signalling when you intend to return.
- ▶ When you go out and about with your laptop, keep it in a nondescript rucksack rather than a special computer bag. Always back up your work onto a floppy disk and keep the disks apart from your computer.

▶ If you use cash-point machines, try to do so during daylight hours, and do not proceed with the transaction if you feel crowded by someone near you or if you notice anything untoward about the machine, such as an unusual device. If concerned, try to use machines inside banks or go with a friend.

▶ Be discreet about using your mobile phone in public places.

If you return home and notice that something is amiss, for example that a window is broken, do not enter the premises. Call the police and wait at a safe distance until they arrive. If you have been burgled, there will be more chance of reclaiming your property if you have marked it with an ultraviolet pen. Your property will be easily identified if marked with your university name and student identification number. Similarly, if you have made a list of your credit card numbers and the emergency numbers for cancelling them, this will ensure that you are able to act quickly in preventing their use by another person. If your mobile phone has been stolen you can render it useless to anyone else by notifying your provider immediately. Call 08701 123 123 to be put through to your provider if you do not know the number (further information can be found on www.immobilise.com).

If you have a car, motorbike or bicycle, you should also take active steps to safeguard it from theft. Cars should always be kept locked and should be parked in busy, well-lit areas if possible. You might also consider fitting a car alarm and a steering lock and etching the vehicle registration number on the windows, headlamps and windscreen. It is unwise to leave valuables in your car, and if you have no choice but to do so, they should be kept out of sight in the boot. The vehicle documents should not be kept in the car as without them it is more difficult for the thief to sell the vehicle (see www.secureyour-motor.gov.uk). If you own a motorbike, you might consider having a combined alarm/immobiliser fitted by an expert and marking the engine and windscreen with the vehicle identification number. Similarly, bicycles may also be marked, and labelled with coded stickers to draw this to the attention of potential thieves. Both bicycles and motorbikes should be locked to immovable objects when you leave them, and all accessories should be removed.

 Insure everything. You can guarantee you will somehow destroy all your possessions in a water fight.

(**Josh**, 3rd-year undergraduate)

▶ Summary

This chapter has shown how you can take control of your health, safety and well-being. It has outlined the importance of registering with a GP and identified what to do if you become ill at university. It has provided initial contact numbers and websites that focus on a wide range of health concerns and presented basic guidelines for healthy eating and food hygiene. It has also shown what you can do to ensure your own personal safety and safeguard your possessions.

▶ More Feedback . . .

❛ *Taking control of my well-being is very hard as I am not a very good cook. I end up eating lots of rubbish all the time! I always feel very weak and without energy if I eat too much rubbish. I did put on a lot of weight in my second year at university when I was buying ready-made food from xxx. They were doing a £5 deal and you could get chips, chickens, ice cream and some other bits. It wasn't very good. All the salt and the fat made me put on weight and I always felt lethargic. It didn't help with my studies. I was fed up with being fat and without energies. I bought myself a cooking book. My secret for healthier eating is to prepare lots of food all together (pasta bake) put it in the fridge and reheat when hungry. Pasta bake can last up to three days (and it will only cost £2 to make!). I also enrolled at the local gym. It is good to exercise at least twice a week. Local gyms always have deals for students and it is another place where it is easy to make friends. With regards to safety, if I go out and come back late, I always get a cab. I get a bus if there are other people that I know with me. I always go out in a group at night. A lot of friends that meet boys at parties always have their phone turned on and via text let the others know where they are going to and with whom. Some of my friends, if they meet a good looking boy worth spending time with, always bring him back to their own flat. It is safer than going to the flat of someone you have just met.* ❜

(**Nicoletta**, 3rd-year undergraduate)

9 Specific Circumstances

This chapter focuses on selected experiences of:

- distance learning students
- disabled students
- international students
- mature students

▶ Distance learning students

For a significant number of students, distance learning represents an attractive way to study for a degree. Instead of enrolling full-time at a university which may be far away, and attending lectures, seminars and tutorials there on a regular basis, distance learning offers the opportunity to study from home. Moreover, as the materials are provided in advance, the student has a great deal of control and autonomy over when to study. There are many distance learning organisations, and procedures and policies may vary from one to another. In this chapter I shall focus on the Open University (OU), as in the UK this is the largest and best-known institution that enables individuals to achieve a bachelor's degree or other qualification (see www.open.ac.uk). The Open University accounts for 22 per cent of all part-time higher education students. It currently has more than 200,000 students including 158,000 undergraduates, and offers a range of 360 courses.

There are several reasons why individuals might choose distance learning. It offers the chance to learn whilst remaining in paid employment; it allows students who may not possess the minimum requirements for traditional university entry to embark upon undergraduate study; it enables people to integrate university study into their everyday lives with minimal disruption, and it provides an opportunity to study for individuals whose circumstances may make learning outside of the home difficult, or who feel more comfortable working in their home environment. These could include carers, parents responsible for young children and some disabled members of the community.

Unsurprisingly, the financial costs of distance learning are considerably lower than those associated with traditional university study. The average cost for an Open University bachelor's degree is £4100, and the average total time taken is six years, although students can take undergraduate courses at a faster or slower pace. There are no residential costs involved apart from voluntary summer school courses, and as individuals are able to undertake paid employment while they are studying, many are able to cover their expenses as they undertake each course. Currently, about 80 per cent of Open University students are learning whilst earning, and, in some cases, their costs are further minimised through sponsorship arrangements with their employer. Means-tested grants are also available for part-time students, including distance learning students.

Financial support for part-time students

A flat-rate grant of £250 to help with course costs was introduced in 2004, supplementing the existing fee support of up to £575 for students on a low income studying at least 50 per cent of a full-time course. However, a new system of fee support came into operation in 2005 linking the level of financial support available to the intensity of study on a sliding scale, with those closer to full-time study being eligible for more funding. Part-time students are entitled to financial support for a maximum of eight years, depending on the length of their course, and certain students may also qualify for assistance from the Access to Learning Fund or their higher education institution. Further information on funding is available from the DfES: telephone 0800 731 9133 or website www.dfes.gov.uk/studentsupport.

Distance learning study

The Open University produces customised textbooks, study packs and course handbooks. In addition, tailor-made television and radio programmes, audio and video tapes, computer software and home experiment kits designed to support the programmes also play an important part in the learning process. Students also receive support and assistance with their studies via personal contact in face-to-face meetings which are generally held on a monthly basis. They are also encouraged to set up their own self-help and support groups with colleagues. The university offers an electronic forum, *First Class*, which may be used to discuss work issues or as a social mechanism for putting people in touch with each other. Non-compulsory summer schools offering intensive teaching for the duration of a week are also available. The OU academic year starts in the spring and runs for ten months, with examinations held in the autumn, and students are offered a range of courses at different levels, together with guidance as to what is required to achieve their goals. In the normal course of events, students start with level one courses and progress to level three. They can take half credits or whole credits towards their degree depending on how much time they are able to allocate to their studies.

It is interesting to note that in recent years distance learning has become more popular amongst young people. Since 1998 the number of students under the age of 24 enrolling with the Open University has tripled and now represents one in ten undergraduates. Professor Allan Cochrane, Pro-Vice-Chancellor (Students) explains this as follows:

> We're finding that the cost of going to other universities is discouraging people and as a consequence they are turning to the OU. When you consider that OU students do not have to find the money to live away from home and that our fees are significantly lower, it is not altogether surprising. An increasing number of people do not want to commit to three years of study before joining the workforce. The Open University allows them to both study and begin their career on completing school or college. They can earn while they learn.[53]

However, there are also disadvantages to distance learning, most notably that interaction between students is limited in comparison with what is available on traditional university courses. Moreover the benefits of 'campus culture' in terms of exposure to a great variety of individuals studying a range of subjects and congregating in key areas of the university are for the most part lacking. Although summer schools do offer a taste of campus culture, they can only offer short-term exposure, and even then, individual circumstances may prevent some students from participating. Although every effort is made to support students and bring them into contact with their peers, inevitably there will be occasions when some students feel isolated.

All university study calls for discipline, self-motivation and good organisational skills. However, for the 80 per cent of students engaged in distance learning whilst undertaking paid employment, these qualities are particularly important as the demands on their time may be considerable. They need to balance the pressures of studying with those of their work, which may not be an easy process. However, several thousands of students graduate successfully each year from the Open University, which is testimony to the value of distance learning.

▶ **Feedback**

> *After I had completed my A-levels I went straight into work without going to university. I got married and had two children and all of a sudden found myself at home with very little to keep my brain active. So I decided to do some studying. I considered some of the courses on offer for mature students, but the childcare facilities available at universities simply did not cater for someone in my position – at the time I had one child at part-time nursery and another at home. It would have meant a huge disruption to the whole family if I had taken that route. I then considered distance learning. For the science course in which I was initially interested there was a 2-hour lecture once a week and the rest of the studying could be done at home, except for one week's residential study. It seemed ideal and I signed up and promptly acquired an enormous tea-chest full of exciting chemicals, glassware, a wonderful kit for making models of molecules, safety goggles and a Bunsen burner. Safety gates kept the children out of the kitchen for an entire year while my chemistry set was in there. I then switched to mathematics for the remainder of my degree. Having studied at home has had some unexpected benefits. My children, who cannot remember a time when Mum was not in a panic about deadlines for homework, or revising madly for one exam or another, are both very interested in science. When it comes to revising before exams they become very focused. They can make up a revision timetable and plan how much time to give to each topic, because they have seen me do it year in, year out. That to me is as big a benefit as finally having a degree. I feel that not only have I engendered in them a love of the study of two fascinating subjects, but I have given them, by example, the mental discipline to make the most of their knowledge when it comes to exam results.*
>
> (**Felicity**, recent graduate)

> *I left school aged 16 with no specific qualifications. I always knew I had it in me to do better so I decided in my mid-20s that I should do a qualification. I thought about O-levels and even A-levels but as I had grown older and I was doing well at work as I had found a good company to work for, then I wondered about a degree. Before too long I had signed up for a foundation course. The first sight of the books was daunting but I was looking*

forward to it – the very fact that you thought you were going to study for a degree was a great feeling. I read the course materials and went to the tutorials and submitted the work – all a bit strange as working full time you have to find a good 10–15 hours a week from your own time to study. [He passed his first two courses.] By now I was flying and thought more about what I wanted to do and signed up for another course – this time in science. I was stumped and struggled really badly as I was hopeless at maths and pulled out a third of the way through. What a shock that was! It made me think that it certainly is not plain sailing and much more thought would be needed on course choice. [He selected other courses and passed.] I hope to obtain my degree this year. Then I may consider honours.

(**Joe**, final-year undergraduate)

I chose to study with xxx [distance learning institution] because it enabled me to study a wide range of subjects from philosophy to ecology. I didn't want to do a straightforward history or biology degree. I wanted to do an assortment of courses. Plus I would have started at a conventional university in 1989 – the first year of student loans, and I did not want to get in debt. I first started distance learning in 1993 but had a break for seven years while my career took off. However, I chose to return [to distance learning] to complete my degree as I travelled overseas a lot with my work so would have been unable to attend regular tutorials.

(**Della**, graduate)

I opted to stop work and stay at home with my children as life was impossible with both of us working. The balls in the air kept falling on the floor and we could not sustain two jobs and look after the kids. However, having changed from a busy job to being stuck at home with young children I was very bored and felt useless. I started a distance learning course in earth science because it was something I'd always been interested in and never had time to do. Studying a completely new area was really exciting and I got positive feedback from the tutor. It made me feel I was engaging with the world outside.

(**Veronica**)

► Disabled students

Disabled students who wish to pursue university study can expect support and assistance so that they are not disadvantaged as a result of their disability. This applies to students with any condition that would pose a barrier to their learning and is therefore a far-reaching declaration. It covers physical disabilities, sensory impairments, chronic conditions, learning disabilities and mental health problems. The Disability Discrimination Act 2002 stipulates that it is unlawful for higher education institutions to discriminate against disabled students and states that the institutions must ensure that disabled students are not disadvantaged. This has resulted in most higher education establishments providing disability advisers and student support staff who are able to offer advice and information, and instigate practical measures to accommodate disabled students throughout the course of their university life. More information about the law is available from the Disability Rights Commission (telephone 08457 622 644 or www.drc-gb.org).

Disabled Students' Allowances (DSAs) are available for full- and part-time higher education students, postgraduate students and distance learning students who meet particular criteria. Each application for DSAs is assessed individually, but the broad guidelines as to what is available may be found in the Government's booklet, *Bridging the Gap: A Guide to the Disabled Students' Allowances (DSAa) in Higher Education*. This is available free of charge from the information line 0800 7319133 or from one of the two following websites: www.dfes.gov.uk/studentsupport/formsandguides/ or www.studentfinancedirect.co.uk. This booklet should be read in conjunction with the Government's publication, *Financial Support for Higher Education Guide*, which is available from the same sources. These brochures cover the situation in England and Wales. Students in Scotland should contact the Students Awards Agency for Scotland (telephone 0845 111 1711 or www.saas.gov.uk) and those in Northern Ireland should contact the Department for Employment and Learning (Northern Ireland) (telephone 028 9025 7710 or wwtv.delni.gov.uk/studentsupport).

The purpose of DSAs is to provide finance to cover extra costs that arise as a direct result of an individual's disabilities. This might include finance for the General Disabled Students' Allowance, money to cover additional travel costs incurred, an allowance for any key specialist equipment that is required, and payment for a non-medical helper. The latter may include note takers, readers, interpreters and other non-medical personnel whose presence enables the student to benefit from his or her course of study. The 2005/6 maximum rates were as follows: specialist equipment allowance for the whole course, £4680; non-medical helper's allowance, £11,840, or £8885 for part-time students; general disability allowance £1565, or £1170 for part-time students. It is worth noting that the DSA will not fund the diagnosis of a disability: however, this is something that the Access to Learning Fund can cover.

DSAs are not means tested and there is no upper age limit. They do not have to be repaid. Each application for a DSA is considered individually by the relevant Local Education Authority (LEA),which will assess whether the applicant is eligible and, if so, how much financial assistance he or she will be given. The relevant form that needs to be completed is the PNI (or PRl if you are a continuing student), and this is available from the LEA or online at www studentfinancedirect.co.uk. Open University students should deal direct with the Open University DSA office.

The onus is on the disabled student to provide evidence of his or her disability. In many cases this will simply require documentation from the person's GP. However, with some learning difficulties, such as dyslexia, the student needs to provide an assessment from an educational psychologist. Neither the LEA nor the OU will finance a diagnosis, so it is the student's own responsibility to ensure that the appropriate assessment has been carried out and the paperwork completed. Unfortunately, this can be costly and can take time. Moreover, for certain conditions, such as dyslexia and dyspraxia, the assessment must be carried out after the person is 16 years of age, and must also be current, as assessments over two years old are considered to be out of date. Skill, the National Bureau for Students with Disabilities, has produced several useful booklets on this subject including *Disabled Students' Allowances*, which identifies the evidence required by LEAs and offers advice on how to make an application. Skill may be reached by telephone from 1.30 p.m. to 4.30 p.m. Monday to Thursday on 0800 328 5050 or via the website www.skill.org.UK. Help and advice is also available from the Disability Advisers within higher education institutions. However, it is important to note that the process of obtaining a DSA can take a long time, particularly if the relevant documentation is not immediately available, so it is wise to anticipate a move to university and start to gather the appropriate paperwork well in advance.

At university, the disability advisers and student support workers can be very helpful both in arranging practical help – such as finding non-medical assistants and ensuring that students with access difficulties are allocated appropriate accommodation~and also ixy providing general advice and information. It is advisable to contact the appropriate staff at your university as soon as possible as establishing a good working partnership will reap dividends in the years to come.

► **Feedback**

> When I applied to study law and Welsh at xxx I was hoping that my disability as a wheelchair user would not hinder my application. At present I am halfway through my degree and ever since I first sent the application my disability has not even been an issue. The university has offered support ranging from suitable accommodation to preferential IT resources and a thorough revision of any exam requirements. Level access to all lecture and tutorial venues I can take for granted and once inside there are tables available for me to work comfortably behind. Some of the higher library shelves are out of reach but other students are always happy to help, not just in the library but also around the campus. My usual response is to politely thank them and carry on alone, but it is nice to know that help is never far away. Not once have I felt it necessary to raise issues with the disability co-ordinators and I am sure the same will apply for the remainder. Life in general in xxx [city] is just as straightforward. You soon learn which places have access and which not to bother with.
>
> (**Geraint**, 2nd-year undergraduate)

> At the age of 50 I viewed myself as a useless burden to myself and to others. Progressive disability – due to fibromyalgia, arthritis and osteoporosis – had forced me to 'retire' from business. Although I had studied to A-level standard in my teens I had been forced to abandon my exams due to ill health. This had aggrieved me throughout life – my friends had their 'piece of paper'!! My husband 'persuaded' me to embark on my first [distance learning] course in 2001. A whole new world opened up for me!!! My dis-abilities would never have allowed me to attend a 'conventional' university but with the xxx university I find I have only 'a-bilities'. Courses are well structured and I can choose what I want to study and when. The support network enables me, even allowing me to sit my exams in my own home with rest breaks included. I am now commencing my fifth year of study and have a few 'pieces of paper' (with more to come)!!! The sense of achievement is unbelievable . . . and I have not even touched on the social aspect – via the conferences – of studying with xxx university!!!
>
> (**Sinead**, distance learning undergraduate)

I have been a student at the University of xxx for three and a half years. As someone who is visually impaired, I feel that it is a very good university to study at. All PCs on the university network are programmed to recognise my user ID so that when I log on JAWS screen-reading software is automatically launched. Using this software I can write assignments, browse the Internet and check e-mails independently. Outside my studies any other department that I have made contact with has been sensitive towards my disability. Because it is such a small campus, it is easy to make friends easily. I am a member of four societies, through which I have made some of my best friends.

(**Den**, final-year undergraduate)

Classes, study, friends, relationships, OCD, having a good time: it is a lot to juggle every day being a student with a 'hidden illness'. Obsessive-Compulsive Disorder [OCD] is a common anxiety disorder where a person has recurrent and unwanted ideas or impulses and an urge or compulsion to do something to relieve the discomfort caused by the obsession. The symptoms feel like a case of mental hiccups that won't go away. OCD decided to 'invade' my life when I was 18. It affects me in that I have fearful thoughts and doubts about whether or not I have done certain tasks. The thoughts and fears can strike at any time and if having a bad day where I am particularly stressed or anxious and the OCD strikes, the only thing I will be able to concentrate on is the OCD fear or doubt. The thoughts can affect and disrupt all parts of my life from studying, going out and even having a chat with a friend. Having OCD has made life difficult at times but has given me a greater understanding of myself. It also led me to make the decision of studying health. I tried to manage the condition alone at first, but it was clear I was struggling. I was handing in assignments late, always stressed, withdrew myself from my friends and my boyfriend, to the point I didn't want to go out anywhere. When it reached that point, I knew I had to open up about having OCD. The relief after I told my close friends and boyfriend was immense. They all provided me with support and encouragement so I could get my life back on track. I also told my tutors about the OCD. They were lovely about it, really helpful by providing me with extra support enabling me to continue with my studies. My tutors don't make an issue out of the OCD, which makes life a lot easier for me.

(**Niamh**, 2nd-year undergraduate)

' When I first started university life, I was shy and not very out-going. My severe deafness made it hard to communicate in large groups and therefore to join in the hustle and bustle of being in a corridor full of students my age. Going out in that first week and being sociable was a real pain; people my age like to go to clubs and bars and (although I enjoyed the atmosphere very much) it was nearly impossible to communicate in these loud and crowded places. Over time, however, I started to fit in well and enjoy it. People soon realised my difficulty so went out of their way to make me feel comfortable. I soon learnt that being shy at the start of the week was nothing to do with being deaf, but more because I was in a situation with a load of people I didn't know. And as I found out, the whole corridor felt the same. I wasn't any different. Soon being deaf didn't become an obstacle at all. Granted, there were certain situations where I needed help (note taking during my first year, for example). There were also health and safety issues to tackle, such as fire alarms that obviously I would not hear if they went off in the night (the college installed a vibrating fire alarm for me). But things like that built a stronger bond with my roommates. They would be concerned that I was out the building if the alarm went off during the night. Now, as I approach the last semester in univer-sity, I can honestly say that I have enjoyed student life immensely. Being deaf has had its hurdles, but the amount of people that made these hurdles disappear (special needs, lectur-ers, fellow students) soon made me tackle student life just like anyone else. '

(**Dean**, final-year undergraduate)

' I am a full-time electric wheelchair user. I expected some strug-gles, and actually they haven't been too bad. Silly things like when the lift broke down at the end of the day and nobody knew quite what to do. At the time it was a bit panicky but it all got sorted. Once or twice a vehicle (college transport) parked right up next to my vehicle and I couldn't get my lift out till the driver returned. Luckily it was only 15 minutes or so. It's just little awareness things that any uni probably has as it reflects the lack of awareness held within the wider community – things like parking over ramps or in blue badge holder spaces. But my immediate fellow students, lecturers and administrative and support staff, that know my needs, are excellent. I'm enjoying it

at the moment and any problems are challenges to be overcome.
I know that sounds a bit of a cliché but it's true! **,**

(**Josh**, first-year undergraduate)

▶ International students

Many home students find the prospect of adjusting to student life daunting, and for overseas students it can represent an even greater challenge. Non-British students may suddenly be thrust into an unfamiliar setting in which everything is new and different: language; climate; food; social behaviour and etiquette; culture; and even approaches to studying. In addition to this, non-British students need to navigate their way through the university application process and appropriate immigration and financial procedures. This can be very complicated, particularly as the regulations tend to change fairly frequently, and the rules vary according to the applicant's country of origin. Most particularly, immigration requirements and university fees differ considerably for students coming from countries in the EEA (European Economic Area) and for those coming to the UK from countries outside the EEA.

Both the British Council (www.britishcouncil.org.uk) and UKCOSA, the United Kingdom Council on Overseas Student Affairs, now known as the Council for International Education, (www.ukcosa.org.uk), offer guidelines for students coming from overseas to study in the UK together with useful advice on settling in. In addition, information may be found on other specialist sites. If you need to check whether or not you require a UK visa, and how to apply, you can find out on www.ukvisas.gov.uk. The immigration procedure is further explained in UKCOSA's guide, *I Am Coming to the UK to Start My Studies: What Do I Need to Do About Immigration?* which can be downloaded from their website. You can also use the Internet to help you select an appropriate course and institution. Individual prospectuses are available via www.educationuk.org and the British Council's relevant booklets, *Choosing the Right Course* and *Choosing Your Degree Programme and Institution* can be downloaded from their website. These brochures look at the types of courses on offer, the qualifications required to register for them, how to make a good choice and what further action is required. The websites of the institutions you select for further consideration are likely to contain images and links that will enable you to get a 'feel' for the environment, and you can look at an evaluation of the educational provision from the Quality Assurance Agency for higher education. The data arises from QAA inspections and may be viewed under 'review reports' on www.qaa.ac.uk. If you wish to find out the equivalent UK qualifications to the ones you hold from your home country, you can do this by contacting the National Recognition Information Centre for the United Kingdom on www.naric.org.uk.

There is also abundant information available on related issues, such as how much it costs to study and live in the UK, how you might best prepare for the journey, what to expect on arrival at the airport, how to reach your final destination via public transport, and what to expect from leisure and shopping facilities. Two specific publications are *First Steps* and *Studying and Living in the United Kingdom*, both produced by the British Council and available on their website www.britishcouncil.org.uk.

Funding is a complex issue which needs to be investigated thoroughly by prospective students. The British Council, UKCOSA and the Foreign and Commonwealth Office have produced an explanatory document entitled *Sources for Funding for International Students*. This covers the criteria for paying home (local) fees as opposed to overseas fees, the processes involved in getting a grant and the mandatory criteria for applicants, and the financial arrangements applicable specifically to EEA students. It also outlines the different scholarships available together with the application procedures, and contains a list of useful addresses. Many non-British students wish to work while they are in the UK, and they can usually obtain a visa or passport stamp that enables them to take employment for up to 20 hours per week. However, in order to clear immigration procedures successfully, students are expected to show evidence that they can provide the necessary finance to live and study in the UK without relying solely on their income from part-time work. Once again, the situation is different for students from EEA countries, so it is important for each individual to understand his or her position. Further information is available in UKCOSA's guidance notes, *Working in the UK during Your Studies*. Also on the UKCOSA website is information about programmes, exchanges and transnational work placements between specific countries. The relevant booklet is entitled *International Mobility and Exchange Schemes*, and it gives specific details about education and training programmes such as Socrates, Leonardo and Tempus.

Each host organisation in the UK provides support for students who arrive from overseas. There is normally an orientation programme, which includes social events so that students can meet new colleagues, and a welcome pack containing literature on all aspects of life as a non-British student in the UK. In addition, advisers and counsellors are generally available to offer assistance and information. However, despite this, culture shock is almost inevitable for those who have not lived in the UK before. It is surprising how much we all take for granted, in terms of what represents 'the norm', when the evidence suggests that diverse cultures do not have a 'universal' standard, especially in matters of social etiquette and interaction. Cultural awareness from all parties is key to preventing misunderstandings and, with this in mind, both the British Council and UKCOSA have produced guidelines on culture shock for international students and for those working with them. The British Council's booklet, *Feeling at Home*, for example, cautions against stereotyping, and asks a series of questions designed to prompt the reader to think in terms of diverse perspectives. It asks, for example, if readers open a conversation by asking about the other person's health or whether they go straight to the point; and whether, if quoted a price, they accept it as fixed or as the starting point for negotiations.[54] This booklet gives basic information and advice on potential cultural differences in areas such as social interaction, study methods, personal hygiene and religion. UKCOSA's guide, *International Students and Culture Shock*, suggests a model of culture shock that encompasses five distinct phases: honeymoon, distress, reintegratation, autonomy and independence. It tracks the feelings that accompany these phases, linking excitement to the honeymoon period; confusion and isolation with 'distress' and anger with 'reintegration' as the individual concerned rejects the cultural differences. At this point the situation improves as the individual comes to accept cultural diversity and feel more relaxed before eventually actively valuing the differences.

In order to prevent misunderstandings and feelings of isolation, it is important to be aware of potential cultural differences and talk about any areas that appear problematic or confusing. Reading the guides mentioned can help, as can mixing socially with people of all nationalities, including home students, in order to get to know them better and in order to enable them to get to know you. Host is an organisation which promotes international understanding by offering the facility for overseas students to be welcomed into private homes as guests for visits lasting normally between one and three days in locations around the UK. Host may be reached via its website on www.hostuk.org.uk.

It is also important for students and their tutors to liaise and discuss exactly what is required in terms of both approach to study and output, and this varies in different countries. Sometimes students may be unused to interacting with a tutor of a different gender, or they might regard challenging their tutors, or calling them by their first name, as impolite. They may also be surprised by the educational style in UK universities, which often calls for the student to take the initiative in structuring and developing a piece of work with comparatively little supervision. All these issues can be resolved through communication.

The British Council notes that over a quarter of a million international students study in the UK each year.[55] This means that British students have the opportunity of gaining an insight into many other cultures during the course of their own studies, which in turn adds a new dimension to student life and enhances the university experience.

► **Feedback**

❛ I'm from Malaysia originally, but I've moved around quite a bit. I was born in Singapore and then moved back to Malaysia, and then back to Canada, Germany, back to Malaysia, and now I'm here. There isn't so much of a culture shock just because I've been raised everywhere. I love the fact that [London] is so international. You don't really feel homesick here. What took me by surprise was how polite most of them [British] are. They are constantly saying 'please' and 'thank you' and apologising. I'm on a government sponsorship. My scholarship covers tuition. It's actually quite a good deal because they also give me about £—— a month. I can cover the cost of rent and my parents give me a certain amount at the beginning of the year. I do temporary jobs – one-offs to earn a quick sum of money. I've just recently applied for a job to do telephone marketing, so it doesn't take too much time away from studies. In my first year I wasn't very sociable. I would probably describe myself as more of a recluse than anything else. I think I was still really worried about my results. I stayed in. I wanted to get the best grades, and I guess over the years I've realised that as important as grades are, you have to be all rounded to get anywhere. This year I am actually President of the Maths Society, and I've started volunteering for things as well. When I first came here I didn't really like the atti-tude – it seemed a lot greyer. The sky seemed greyer; everything seemed a lot duller, but after being here for two or three years I don't actually want to leave now. I am hoping to find a job here next year. ❜

(**Azura**, Malaysian student)

❛ Language was definitely one of the things that gave me a hard time here. Although my friends respected me, I still felt sort of inferior in front of native speakers, since what they knew about my thoughts was what I was able to express in this language, which was quite limited and not what I was really able to think. Another point is that people expect you to speak English in this *country. People don't expect you to speak Bulgarian in Bulgaria or Turkish in Turkey. On the contrary, from my experience, in very touristy places in Greece even Greeks have to order in English in cafés. I would say that English people expect you to speak English almost everywhere. How often do they try to learn some basic expressions in a foreign language when they visit a place as tourists?*

(**Despina**, Greek student)

When I arrived, I was really depressed; everything was so difficult to do on my own. I was homesick for about two weeks, but fortunately I was not alone. Then things were better. I met some nice Erasmus students and parties began! During the first lectures I had great difficulty to understand the teachers; they were speaking so quickly. Studying in xxx is really different; here lecturers are more distant; during the lectures there is no real communication with the students; nobody ever asks questions, work is definitely individual. However, the tutorials were really good; my tutor was so nice. He tries to speak slowly to make us understand. But life is so expensive. I have euros and not pounds, and each transaction I make I have to pay some service commissions, so it became more expensive. I sought to open a bank account here but there were more problems than solutions. Getting used to the climate was hard. I'm so used to warmth and sun, but fortunately we have some really nice weather in xxx, except the cold. I'm not pessimistic about my year in xxx. I saw so many things and I learnt to be independent. That's a very rich experience and I have no regrets.

(**Marie-Hélène**, French student from Reunion Island)

I think overseas students can have difficulties getting used to different study skills that are required in the UK. The 'Confucian belt' approach and others is to sit and wait for the professor or the lecturer to tell them what to do, and to cast the pearls before them if I can put it as extremely as this, and their job is to pick up enough of these to pass the exams to get the qualification; whereas the UK approach expects them to develop into the self-learning position, so they can actually be self-reliant in educational terms. So there is that transition which can be difficult for UK students as well, but if you have been brought up in a much more, shall we say, authoritarian stratified education or regime then that change could be quite difficult. The other thing I think is the approachability, because there are groups where the idea is that you walk into a lecture or a class and you listen to the person who then leaves, whereas here the staff are accessible. But they don't say: 'Come and see me'. They will expect the student to come to them, which again is not a very easy thing to do if you have not been brought up in that educational system.

(**Tom**, tutor)

Leaving home was very difficult at the beginning, but after four months, I became stronger and more independent. Life is very expensive in xxx, especially for European students. The money is not the same and sometimes it's difficult. I chose to live in xxx because it's less expensive than in the city centre, but it's a bit far and when I want to go to the city centre it costs a lot. At night, it's not safe at all when I go out and I have to take the bus. People are strange and drunk. I don't feel secure.

(**Françoise**, French student from Reunion Island)

The first thing that came to mind when I was asked about 'student life in the UK' was 'tutorial', as all the university lecturers who taught me in my home country were seen as distant so that I found it difficult to approach and even talk about my study in general, let alone my personal problems. I felt really strange to call my tutor by his first name and having a regular private meeting based on 'face-to-face' communication was and still is challenging. As I got used to this rather personalised teaching-and-learning system, I have realised that most of the benefit comes not from the course itself but from the framework it creates – a space to think about and discuss issues, a chance to explore new areas and to be inspired not only by tutors but also by other like-minded students.

(**Mi-Rim**, Korean student)

International students share the same general academic concerns as 'home' students as well as many others that compound with one another in ways that potentially affect academic success and overall quality of life. Aside from the obvious differences in weather, language, expenses, accommodation, education systems, racial majority, limited contact with friends and family, there are a host of socio-cultural aspects about *studying in the UK such as gender and class expectations; styles of written, verbal, and non-verbal communication (especially with authority figures like lecturers, advisers); time management; coping strategies; accessing available resources, etc. I have found this to be true even for those of us from English-speaking countries in North America and the Caribbean. In the student housing I lived in, the trend was that the home students formed their own social circles that excluded international students and revolved around the notorious drinking culture in the UK. International students therefore may have to try a bit harder to make friends, especially friends from the UK, than they would otherwise. I find the UK superficially multi-cultural in practice and more hierarchical/classist than many places. What I mean is that yes, there are plenty of international folks represented in the UK but not too much 'genuine' social mixing whether it be in various neighbourhoods, council estates, workplaces, pubs, school, etc. In fact I have witnessed and overheard several incidents/comments that were racist/ethnocentric and unnecessarily rude or hurtful in and out of academic institutions right here in this city. But at the end of the day, weather and day-to-day expenses aside, I would still decide to study in the UK because it is overall faster (degrees are about a year or more shorter in duration than most other parts of the world), cheaper, and more flexible for me to do so than in the USA believe it or not . . . (especially at Ph.D. level) and there aren't many other parts of the (English speaking) world where one can earn an internationally recognised degree.*

(**Ariana**, Greek–American student)

▶ Mature students

Anyone who has already had their twenty-first birthday before starting their undergraduate course is classed as a mature student. For funding purposes, a further distinction is made if the individual fulfils the criteria to be classified as an independent student. In this case the student's own financial situation is assessed and his or her parents are not expected to contribute to university fees or living costs. To achieve independent student status, a person must either be over 25 years old, or have been married for two years, or have been self-supporting for three years prior to the start of the academic year in question.

Mature students have similar entitlements to younger students in terms of assistance with tuition fees and the Higher Education Grant, and those up to the age of 50 may get a student loan. Childcare grants and assistance from university funds may also be available for full-time students meeting the appropriate criteria. As each individual presents a different set of circumstances, identifying specific entitlements is not always a quick task. The best course of action is to read through the relevant literature and seek advice and clarification from the relevant information lines if necessary. The DfES produces several relevant free guides which provide further information on these matters, including *Financial Support for Higher Education Students* and *Childcare Grant and Other Support for Student Parents in Higher Education*. These may be obtained by telephoning the DfES information line on 0800 731 9133. You may also find it helpful to check out the following websites: www.dfes.gov.uk and www.aimhigher.ac.uk. Students living in Scotland seeking information about the Mature Students Bursary Fund should contact the Student Awards Agency for Scotland, www.student-support-saas.gov.uk. The equivalent contact for students living in Northern Ireland is the Department for Employment and Learning, www.delni.gov.uk/studentsupport.

At first glance, the specific circumstances of a group of mature students may appear very different. Typically, an intake of mature students may include people in their early twenties who may or may not have left the parental home; individuals with children or other adults who are financially dependent on them; middle-aged people; and pensioners. Whilst their lives may outwardly differ considerably, it is nevertheless likely that there is significant common ground, too.

Most mature students have life experience gained from paid or unpaid employment in the outside world. To a greater or lesser degree, they have generally had the opportunity to hone their skills, identify their strengths and improve on their weaknesses in the workplace or the world at large. They may also have practical experiences that they can now draw on such as working as part of a team, giving presentations and researching new areas. With life experience comes confidence, and mature students may be less daunted by the new university environment and their dealings with the staff than their younger counterparts. It has also been observed that mature students often tend to cope well with the workload and produce a high standard of output. One reason for this could be that they are well practised in time management and self-discipline and are realistic about the demands of the course. However, mature students may not have been in a learning environment for a considerable time prior to starting at university. This can make progress feel slow in the initial weeks and can affect an individual's self-confidence and self-esteem. Interaction with younger students can be very helpful as each party can benefit from the other's experience and outlook. Younger students who have recently completed an A-level in your subject may also be able to help in navigating reading lists, putting books in order of priority and deciphering new jargon.

It is also helpful to share experiences with other mature students, who may be better placed to understand the specific stresses and pressures involved than younger students. Sometimes discussing a potential problem, such as how to balance childcare and study responsibilities during school half-terms, can be very helpful, as others may have already found a solution to a particular dilemma. It is a good idea to discuss anything that may potentially pose an obstacle to studying with the relevant tutor, as he or she is likely to have come across the situation before and may be able to make practical suggestions. Some appointments, for example, can be rescheduled to more convenient times, and it is often possible to obtain permission to take older children into the university library or to lectures.

It is important that mature students do not assume that they cannot play an active role in student social life simply because they may not be inclined to join in with clubbing and drinking activities. There is likely to be a wide range of societies and organisations at the university and generally most tastes are catered for. If not, it is worth considering starting a new club as the social opportunities and the chance to meet people from a wide variety of backgrounds and cultures is one of the key benefits associated with student life.

▶ Feedback

> ❛ As a 'mature' student – which is a bit of a joke because I'm 24! – really research whether there are going to be any people your own age, because it's quite a shock when everyone in your lecture is 18. ❜
>
> (**Helen**, 2nd-year undergraduate)

> ❛ I chose to live on campus because I want my time at university to be as straightforward, and as focused, as possible. I want to be immersed not just in academic life, but in all the other things that university offers, to be part of the university 'village'. A handful of older students also live in halls and they are mostly international postgraduates. This mix of living among school leavers and students with a diverse range of languages and interests makes life after lectures really interesting. While I am old enough to be a

parent to most of my cohort, this doesn't make any difference to them and I am treated without prejudice. This has been a pleasant and welcome surprise, and all of it challenges my perceptions of modern education – and students! I sometimes miss older conversation, but the greater difference is in the seminars. Although I bring a wider context of knowledge and experience, younger undergrads bring a fresher perspective. At times it can be frustrating when some students don't bother with the preparation for lectures, but as term progresses peer group pressure soon sorts out those who want to be here, and those who don't. The biggest disappointment is that the social life for older students isn't really catered for as most mature students live off campus; all the union events are geared towards younger students, and this is a national trend not unique to my university. I would have no hesitation in recommending study to anyone, of any age. Things have changed, in many respects for the better, and higher education is very accessible now for older learners. '

(**Stephen**, 1st-year undergraduate)

' *I started my BA Cultural Studies course as a mature student out of interest and to provide a different focus from my work as an IT manager. Over the years it reinforced my belief that I would like to change career path at some point. Two years ago I took voluntary redundancy, which gave me the opportunity to do what I wanted. I initially went to Mongolia for three months. Whilst there, as so often happens in life, a new opportunity arose to become a United Nations Volunteer. The whole experience was excellent! It has reaffirmed a new career direction and I have now returned to complete my studies. Be warned, whatever stage you are in life, study may well change your life completely . . . but for the better.* '

(**Nicholas**, undergraduate)

' *Mature students can suffer all the same difficulties as younger students, but because they often have responsibilities towards other people in their lives, particularly children and partners, they may also have specific pressures on their time and attention which younger students don't have. They need to make tutors aware immediately if something has gone wrong which leads to absences, such as childcare arrangements falling apart or a child being ill. The lecturer then at least knows that the student might need an extra tutorial to discuss what they have missed. They also need to set up a support network amongst their fellow students, mainly a reliable colleague in every class who will collect handouts and communicate information about assignments etc. I have had many years' experience of teaching Access students who will go to university if they pass the Access course. The most consistent factor has been the tremendous lack of confidence such students suffer. Once a student even had to check whereabouts on the paper she should write her name when we were doing a written class exercise because she didn't trust herself to make this small decision. Tutors need to be aware of this low self-esteem, but students should also realise that they bring much of value to their studies because they are mature and they are usually well-motivated, having overcome many difficulties in order to even begin their return to study. I think it is vital that students realise that whatever problems they had before they came on the course will still be there once they are on the course. They must be realistic about what they can cope with, discussing their situation with the course tutor during the application process and taking their return to study in small steps.*

(**Jo**, tutor)

I chose to come back to university after a life-threatening illness. As I'm in my forties I wanted to do something I felt would benefit me. I considered that I was very lucky to have one of the best universities within my home town. For me, returning to study and learning to do things academically have not been easy, but everybody is very helpful and I'm really enjoying my time at university. I think it is harder to sustain friendships as the majority of people are a lot younger than I am, but I have joined the Mature Society, and I'm looking forward to their events.

(**Chris**, 1st-year undergraduate)

When I attended interview for my place at university my fellow interviewees were ranged from 21 to 50 plus; when I took up my place I was, at 37, the oldest undergraduate in my college. There were so many things dividing me from my fellow students: a family; a home to run; my age, and the life I had led to get there. I found myself sitting on the stairs at my first college bop thinking 'what the hell am I doing here?' while people surged all around me drinking and dancing the night away. Then I got talking to someone; got up; joined in and had a ball. It seemed I was the only one bothered by my age – the only criterion for fitting in is joining in. And the question 'what am I doing here?' is not the sole prerogative of the mature student. In reality we know, with greater clarity, what we are doing there: we really want to study our subject! Mature students have a reputation for working hard: unsurprising given the commitment needed to go back into full-time education. I had another reason: I doubted my ability to absorb information and pass exams. Some of my hard work was driven by fear! Whether through a real engagement with my subject or sheer fright, I got my degree and I would recommend the experience to anyone.

(**Miranda**, recent graduate) **'**

10 Students' Experiences

This chapter offers an insight into student life from the perspective of eleven current undergraduates studying a range of subjects at various UK universities.

▶ Marina

Marina is 21 years old and is studying to become a doctor.
'When opting for my university courses I have to admit that it was partly ones I really wanted to go to and partly ones I thought I could get into. There are two main types of course [if you wish to read medicine]: the more academic traditional ones in which you do three years of science and then you have the clinic years in which you learn in the hospitals. The second type is the problem-based learning, with students being more medically based at the beginning, with contact with hospitals (not that we go as often as expected). This often involves learning medicine around the different systems such as the cardiovascular system or the respiratory system. I didn't want the traditional course. I also had to think about universities' views of gap years.' [Marina applied for courses offering clinical experience from the outset, and she selected larger universities on the basis that she had more chance of getting in.]

'As a boarding school girl, settling in [to uni] didn't involve many problems – no homesickness and no feelings of it being strange having so many people around. Also having taken a gap year helps you to grow up and get on well on your own. You can tell the gap year students – not as fresh and naïve. I settled in quickly. The halls had long corridors and so I left my door open and met new people as they arrived. The one thing I was worried about was getting back into work, which I did find difficult and think I have been struggling with ever since.'

'Freshers' week [involved] some good parties and some not so good ones. Getting to grips with where places were, buying tickets beforehand (as someone who doesn't organise too far in advance), was odd. I met a million people doing all sorts of courses; all the obvious questions of name, course, gap year [came up] – all of which you don't really remember, especially as a lot of alcohol is consumed. On our floor we drank a 1.5 litre bottle of vodka in the first few days, had to replace it and finished that too (I haven't really drunk vodka since then). I was the only person organised enough to bring alcohol with me – very important especially when new, as it's sociable. I brought the vodka and six bottles of wine and was very glad of them.'

'As a gap year student, I couldn't really remember a lot of my sixth-form work, but in the first term it was quite a lot of sixth-form work taken just a little bit further. That and 10 o'clock Monday morning dissections thrown in which was very different from anything I'd done at school. A few people had some problems but everyone does get used to it and it is fascinating to see what people's organs actually look like in comparison to what you have previously believed. There are quite a few new terms to get to grips with in anatomy before you even learn the parts. It's a shock when you realise you are using the terms in everyday life. As long as you keep on top of the work it isn't too much of a problem.'

'Budgets – I'm hopeless at money and I'm afraid I can't deal with it. All I know is that after six years I'm going to be very in debt. I have my student loan and the rest I make from working and my dad helps me with the difference. I just try to spend as little as possible and I'm not very extravagant. Last year I had saved enough from my year off to support myself through the whole year. Unfortunately this year is not the same. As a student you learn that taking the bus is cheaper and where to hunt for cheaper drinks, food etc.'

'There are always going to be people you love and some you hate. The rooms [in the hall of residence] weren't particularly lovely but perfectly liveable in, with space to put all my junk. The kitchen was a disaster area. I hated it. People definitely weren't used to not having their mums around to clean up after them. We ended up having a box in which all the dirty stuff got put and left. It was foul! You have to get used to being woken up from time to time and the fire alarms in the middle of the night drove us mad. But then again it's great to have so many people around to talk to and go out with, and the likelihood of finding someone going home to your halls on a night out is quite high. Also, having six medics on the floor is a bonus as there will be someone to explain things, borrow books from or tell you where you are supposed to be. Medics do often become a bit cliquey, mainly as we are there for six years and many people don't want to hear about the inside of someone's body or the fantastic growth you saw that day.'

'This year I live with five of us from our halls. The house is 20 minutes' walk away from uni. I don't really see a lot of my housemates sometimes as

I'm out at rowing, but we all rub along OK. As it is owned by my friend's mother we have it a bit easy with all bills inclusive and a tumble dryer. Once again my biggest complaint is the state of the kitchen which I spend ages cleaning, but that is really all part of living with other people, I suppose. Accommodation is expensive, which is important when applying. I'm paying nearly double what some of my friends are elsewhere. If taking a six-year course this will definitely add up and people must be prepared for this.'

▶ Jools

Jools has first-hand experiences of the difficulties of living on a tight budget.
Jools is 18 and is in her first year studying drama production with media studies and creative writing. She opted for a place in a hall of residence on the advice of her friends and does not regret this decision: 'It's such a laugh. It's like being on holiday.'

She enjoys her course and living at university but almost from the outset Jools ran into financial difficulties. Her parents are not in a position to help with her tuition fees or living costs and she is reliant on a loan to meet her costs. However, the loan does not cover tuition fees plus living expenses, and Jools inadvertently compounded the situation when she first arrived at university by going out frequently. She recalls that 'we all spent a fortune in the first week' and that for the first two weeks she and the others in her hall went out every night. Although she was not wildly extravagant, she was nevertheless living beyond her means, and this rapidly became apparent.

'Everyone told me how hard student life would be: I'd have no money, have to budget, be sensible with my money etc . . . but I really didn't listen. I wish I had though because two months into my first year I'd already spent my entire loan and even gone over my overdraft limit which is nearly £1250 and maxed out my credit card (£500). Now I'm really struggling to live and have nothing at all to show for it. I literally xxxxxx it all up against a wall. The only advice I have, and I know it's a cliché, is to be really careful with your money – write down *everything* you buy – even a can of pop! And *don't* get credit cards/store cards – the interest is so high. I'm going to be paying it off for years.'

Having taken stock of the situation, Jools set about remedying it. She photocopied her CV and distributed it widely in the area near to the university. As a result she found a job behind the bar in a local nightclub and she now works there twice a week. She also took to writing down everything that she spent money on in order to see where it was going, and is careful not to buy anything unnecessary. She still goes out with her friends, but now they have a few drinks at home before leaving, and just buy one or two while they are out, as drinking at home is considerably cheaper. She and her flat-mates sometimes play drinking games with the people in the neighbouring flat.

Despite the problems caused by her financial situation, Jools really enjoys student life and considers her first term at university to have been 'amazing'.

▶ **Jeremy**

Jeremy is Malaysian and is in his third year, studying mechanical engineering.

Jeremy came to the UK because he believed that 'graduates from overseas, preferably the UK or the US or Australia, have much better opportunities back home'. He is financing his studies with a loan from the Malaysian government. 'I have to pay it back. It's a special loan in the sense that you don't get interest. It's a huge debt. I'm not actually thinking about it right now, but it shouldn't be a problem because if I do go back I'll most probably get a better job, and the instalment that we have to pay back is quite small and over a long period. So it's usually not too bad.'

'I think cost is one of the important things. I think it's quite difficult for a lot of international students to fully experience coming overseas mainly because of the cost, mainly tuition fees. If you want to travel somewhere you need to pay for transport. And to do that you need to work. I do know people who work a lot, just to support themselves, at least for living fees, so they work the maximum of 20 hours per week. But it does affect study so you have to choose. I'm quite lucky to get the loan. Some of them don't. During term time last year I worked in the union café as a waiter for three hours a week. In the summer I worked as an administrative assistant in the international office. I loved it. It was fun. It was a great summer. I would recommend students to stay back over summer. It's the best time to stay back in the UK. There is no problem with the weather; there are plenty of things to do; the sun is up to ten. In Malaysia, you get sun the whole year round, every day, so there is quite a difference.'

'People here are really friendly. It's what I noticed when I first came here. If you talk to them they will talk back to you whereas back home if you talk to someone they will think: "Why is this stranger talking to me?" Not that approachable! The culture back home is that it can take a bit of time to warm up to strangers. The wonderful thing is that in the first term at university everyone comes with one thing in mind which is to make new friends, so that really makes everything easier, for international students as well. Languagewise – it wasn't perfect when I first came. When I first came I think I found it difficult hearing – it's the tone – and when I spoke people did not really understand me. At the start I had to really concentrate, but after a month or two I got used to it.'

'I think the approach to study [is different]. The lecturers here don't spoon-feed you. They give you a bit of a clue and then you need to go back and figure it out. It comes down to a lot of hard work by yourself trying to figure things out. Attending tutorials and questioning. People here question a lot. It's slightly different back home. The teachers don't really promote question-ing. I don't think it's because they don't want to. It's just that they aren't used to it. It's the culture back home. It's the big difference. So when we come over here we don't really ask many questions.'

'In the first year we get to live in halls because it's easier for us as it's our first time [in the UK]. [Now] I rent from a private landlord. It's a two-bedroom flat, so two bedrooms plus the living room for three of us. And we share the kitchen and the bathroom. The thing with living in halls is other people get quite dirty. So especially for us, because it's really expensive to live out, international students tend to eat at home. We tend to cook by ourselves. So the kitchen is quite an important place to us. Most of us usually go back in the summer because it's cheaper to fly back than to stay on. Things here are really expensive if you're not working here. If we go back in the summer, we usually come back with a full load of stuff. Usually it's Malaysian ingredients because we have a wide variety and because we cook a lot.'

'Ideally I would like to work here for a few years and then go back. It's best if I can bring back some experience of working in the UK back home.'

▶ Nicoletta

Nicoletta has experience both of commuting to university from home and of flat-sharing.
Nicoletta is Italian, but she moved to the UK on her own when she was 18, and four years later decided to go to university. Originally, her intention was to commute to university so she only considered those within reasonable travelling distance. 'I was not looking to move into student accommodation. My aim was to get a degree and meet new people. I was not escaping from home (I had already done that), I was not looking forward to having a student loan (I had been working for four years so I was actually worried about being a student) and wanted to get a good degree.'

'When I started my course I expected the university to be more organised.

However, all large organisations have issues with managing their resources. I am happy with the majority of my teachers (there were a couple of foreign teachers hard to understand) and like the coursework. I have met teachers that really inspire me and that make me want to do well. In my three years I have came across some exceptional teachers. They treat you like an individual. I found some of them very approachable and understanding. I feel that, in the majority of the cases, if there is a problem I can speak to them. However, a lot of people in my class (but I know other people on other courses have done the same) soon realised that they could come up with some problems (porkies of course!) and get the teachers' sympathy and possibly an extension on their work. I hate that. They make us all look like a bunch of lazy people always asking for a little extra time (but they are always in the library talking rubbish and downloading music on the Internet . . .).'

'In my second year at university I decided I had enough of travelling on the train [and] I moved [in] with another girl from my course to [within] walking distance of the university. This became my new home. I chose an area that is safe and that I liked. I chose wisely who to share with, as being friends and living together are two different things. It is hard to get used to other people's habits . . . I budgeted carefully but I moved in with someone that was struggling with money! It is not nice to know your flatmate can't pay the bills! I made sure that the person I was moving in with was similar to me. We established a few easy-to-follow house rules on cleaning, noise and having guests. My move with my friend worked out OK although she left at the end of the contract, as she couldn't afford it anymore.'

'It makes a real difference if the university is set in a nice, vibrant place. The area is gorgeous, bars, pubs, park and so on . . . I thought that by being closer to university I would have had a chance to participate more in students' activities (going to the bars, karaoke, sports) but it didn't really happen. It is an expensive area and I have to work twice a week. The rest of the time I spend studying and preparing essays. At the weekend I always spend time with my boyfriend who wouldn't be really impressed if I proposed to go to the student union bar for a drink. Besides, none of the friends I made at university participate in student union activities. They all work, have a boyfriend that does not go to university and are a bit older! (I will be 25 soon – the other girls are 29 and 27).'

'Managing a budget can be hard whilst at university. There are a lot of people out there that have just left home for the first time in their life, and are given a £5000 student loan. They go mad, shopping, drinking and more . . . Then they run out of money and they start eating beans on toast. I never had to do that. I always worked and spent my student loan wisely (it's very hard to manage your student loan – but definitely possible!). In the summer I always find a full-time job and save a bit of money. I am a shopaholic and I will always be, but during my university time I have been doing a lot of window-shopping instead. You learn to do it. It is a small price to pay to be educated to a higher level.'

'It is also important to have some generous friends! I am honest when I go out and say to my friends that I can only spend £20 for the whole evening. People really do understand and buy me a drink or two. Christmas? Birthdays? I don't buy any presents. Cards will do. I hate being mean but this is part of managing a small amount of money that must last over a long period. When I am asked what I want for Christmas I always ask for vouchers. I can buy food, clothes, underwear, soap, tights, socks and so on . . . If I don't need anything in particular then I ask for presents like perfumes and accessories. (This sounds so calculating, I am sorry!)'

'There is a difference about studying at school and studying at university. At university you are more independent. What a lot of people, including myself, find hard is to manage all the spare time that is available. A lot of us get carried away chatting, listening to music, going to the gym rather than actually reading and working on essays . . . Time management is a must-have skill. It is important for me to have a day schedule, knowing what I will be doing throughout the day. I follow my daily plan and get done all the tasks I need to complete. I feel a lot better at the end of a day when I have completed all my tasks.'

▶ Anthony

Anthony is a mature, disabled, distance learner.
Anthony describes himself as a '44-year-old disabled male who is classed as unfit for work'. He lost two fingers in an industrial accident, and the bones in a third finger fused, causing nerve pain, which has since increased considerably, leading to periods of incapacity. He also suffers from depression.

'I started to study with the xxx university [distance learning institution] in 1999 as a way to give my mind some cerebral exercise. I chose to study mathematics as it has always been a subject I find interesting. My main reason at the time was to simply study as a way to do something other than do nothing. I did not even think of the social side of student-hood and I certainly did not think of a degree at the end of it. I chose to study with the xxx university rather than a conventional university because of the advantage home study afforded. The chances of my being unable to attend regular lectures at a conventional university made it apparent I was not going to be successful if I chose that route.'

'In the beginning I made it clear to the university that I am disabled and that handwriting was not easy due to the nature of my disability, meaning that I need to produce all my work on a computer but found a problem in the production of diagrams and graphs on the computer. I was able to produce these by hand but found it very difficult and painful. The university received the medical evidence they asked for and were happy with my requests for help. This was mainly in the timing of assignments.'

'In the second year there was an examination which the university attempted to adapt to my requirements with the use of a computer that I could not use due to hand problems, and an amanuensis who was not able to write what was required and resulted in my having to teach the person how to produce the answers I needed recording. This resulted in a few forms being submitted relating to these difficulties and the Students Association taking up the issue and lobbying on the issue. Since then I have used an amanuensis for each examination and while this is not ideal it is better than the alternative of trying to do the work by hand (an almost impossible task).'

'Socially I was inactive (so to speak) in the first 18 months but accepted an invite to attend a meeting of the regional group within the Students Association where I found I was welcome, and decided to volunteer to represent my fellow students.'

'The university uses the Internet as a contact medium. In fact to be more specific it uses its own intranet system for students to contact each other on a vast variety of topics such as study, branch business and a large variety of other topics including disabilities, sports, animals and many others. This intranet system is the campus, campus bar, meeting rooms, coffee shop etc. (so to speak), where students can meet up to chat. It is the glue that binds a lot of the students together and helps in more ways than just study.'

'The cons of distance learning are as follows: motivation is a lot more relevant in that you need to be able to self-motivate yourself to do the work required. You are usually on your own physically so do not have anyone to bounce ideas off as in a classroom and this can demotivate. Other things can distract you, such as daily life, and this can cut into the time you put aside for study.'

'The pros of distance learning for me are as follows: time commitment is flexible so that pain-related problems can be eliminated by working round them. I do not have to be in a classroom eight hours a day five days a week. I can work as fast or as slow as I want to. I do not have to travel to a classroom every day. Tutorials are held locally. You can study anywhere you want to – just pick up a book and go. You can work and study, so reducing the problems that work (earn money to live) or study (do not earn money) cause.'

▶ **Catherine**

Catherine has experience of living at home throughout university.
'I'd always associated university with having to live away from home, but when the time came to move away I really didn't feel ready or entirely happy with my choice of course. I cancelled my university applications and reapplied to go to a university where I would be able to remain living with my parents, to study English, mainly because I didn't really know what else to do.'

'I was concerned about being a home student as I'd heard loads of stories about people who had always felt left out and who didn't fully enjoy their time at uni, and for the first few weeks this did seem to be the case: I didn't attend any Freshers' events because I hadn't met anybody yet, and during the first week of lectures I felt quite intimidated by the groups of 'new best friends' and the stories of halls and fresher parties etc. There didn't seem to be much provision (well, any at all) made for people who didn't live in student accommodation. I did start to notice, though, that a lot of friendships were superficial and that people were only talking to so many others because they were under pressure to make friends, whereas I still had a circle of friends at home. Once I relaxed and realised it was only me that was alienating myself, it was easy to make friends and to become involved.'

'Whereas people in student accommodation can easily meet up with other students, it takes me an hour to get to uni (a combination of trains and walking) and just over that to get to my friends' student houses, and so it's unrealistic for me to go out as much as other people. On saying that, I do find myself often using the commute as an excuse to be lazy and just see people from home, and so sometimes I say yes to things that I can't really be bothered doing, just so I'm seeing people and maintaining friendships, whereas other people can do that by popping next door for a cup of tea. In the second year I split up with my boyfriend and some friends from home moved away, so I felt a lot more pressure to make more of my uni friendships, and as a result I am a lot closer to people at uni now as I see them as proper friends, not just as people to sit in lectures with and go on the occasional night out. People know it costs me £13 to get home in a taxi and that sleeping on someone's floor is not great, so I don't think anyone thinks any less of me just because I don't go out as much. It's just a case of knowing that uni is what you make of it, and that you will only be really disadvantaged as a home student if you let it be that way.'

'I think there's a great pressure on students to make their university years the best of their life and that this automatically means you need to live in a grubby student bedsit and have no money, just for the "experience". I know

now, from seeing how my friends live, that I wouldn't want to live like that. Living at home means I have been able to keep my Saturday job from school and have absolutely no debt. I have quite a bit of money left over from my year out (I worked full-time) and together with my ten hours a week (which gives me about £240 a month), I don't really need student loan money. My parents pay for my tuition fees and give me about £30 a week as extra, so I am really lucky. I'm only in uni a few hours a week, so transport costs are low, and I only need 2 glasses of wine and am well on my way, so nights out with me are very economical!'

'I live in a clean house, do minimum housework, and have peace and quiet to do my work, as well as never having to rely on dodgy library printers. Yes, I do feel I've missed out a bit socially, and that I'd love to have loads of stories about my crazy house nights out, but I think I'm too independent and need my own space too much to really feel happy in a student house.'

'Whether you're a home student or not, it is difficult adjusting from a sixth-form style of working to that at university. I was used to being at the top of my class in sixth form, and so it was quite difficult attending seminars where a lot of the work just flies over your head, and a lot of people are much more intelligent that you are. Because my sixth form was part of my school, I was still babied a lot, and so it was really difficult knowing how much reading was enough, how much revision to do, and what was expected of me. I ended up doing far too much work and reading articles for the sake of it, just because I wasn't used to being able to manage my own time. You get used to doing work every night at sixth form and it takes some getting used to when you discover that you can pretty much do as much or as little as you want at uni, and that no one is really going to chase you up about it. I've always been quite good at motivating myself so this wasn't a problem for me, but I know it can really make others stop making an effort and not get the results they probably could. The library can be a nightmare sometimes because every-one's scrabbling after the same book and if you can't do the main reading for the topic, the essay's going to get a lower mark. Once you've got the reading though, I've found it's a lot more relaxed than at sixth form, and if you don't make effort one term or on one essay, you can make up for it next time without hassle from lecturers.'

'I would never, ever put people off living at home, and neither would I totally recommend it; it's a really personal choice and I know that I'd regret having spent over £10,000 on a three-year experience, but at the same time I do feel that others have got more out of it than I have.'

▶ **Emily**

Emily is the first member of her family to go to university.
Originally, Emily didn't particularly want to go to university because 'My parents had never been; friends had never been, and I didn't know anyone or anything.' However, she decided to put in an application and review how she felt about it nearer the time. 'I went through all the prospectuses. I knew I didn't want to be more than two hours away from home so that narrowed it down. And then, I didn't really want to be in a city because I've always been used to living in the countryside.' Emily only applied to two universities and didn't attend open days. However, when she went for her first interview she was very disappointed: 'It was horrible. It looked very square, very dark.' Fortunately, she was impressed by her alternative choice and 'felt like I could be there'. Having deliberated at some length, Emily opted to take a three-year degree that would enable her to work as a primary school teacher immediately after graduation, as she did not want the added expense of a PGCE, and sought the security of an assured job on graduation together with help in finding it.

When the time came to go to university, only a few of Emily's friends took up their places: 'Of all those who applied, there was only a handful of us who actually went. The rest of them backed out and said: "No I'm too frightened. I don't want to go." A lot of them have just done nothing. They haven't even got jobs.'

When she left home for the start of the first term, Emily felt very nervous. 'Mum and Dad took me. Everyone kept saying goodbye which was horrible. I didn't know what I was expecting myself, so I didn't want them to say anything.' Her parents drove her to her hall of residence and then left. 'The first few days felt like a lifetime because you don't know anyone. The first thing you know you've got to do is just open your door and just start speaking to these people. There's 18 to a corridor and everyone is in the same position. Nobody knows anyone and everyone is really scared. We were all in the corridor after our parents had left, and you just introduce yourself – your name, what course you do – it's all the same questions. Making friends was the hardest bit, because you didn't know anyone's personality. And you held yourself back a lot. You didn't reveal too much about yourself. And we went for a drink every night for about the first month and I'm not used to doing that. I'm not used to drinking alcohol every time I go out because I usually drive. You felt you had to have something alcoholic otherwise you weren't cool. Everyone just kept drinking, getting drunk every night.'

However, as time passed, Emily came to enjoy living in the hall of residence. Moreover she realised that she was lucky to have a place there as she had previously been told by administrative staff that live-in places were over-subscribed and some new students would have to wait for places until others dropped out: 'They said: "Up to a hundred people will drop off your course within the first month." So I was like, "Oh Gosh, I hope one of them is not me!"'

Although the showers 'got really gross', and 'the fire alarm went off about twice every single night at two and about four or five in the morning' as drunk residents set it off, other aspects of hall life were very appealing: 'It's an experience that you won't forget, and it's where you create your best friends. You could make a social life as well which I wasn't used to doing. It's nice for your first year and I enjoyed it right up until the end, but you then get to that point where you want your own kitchen with less [people]. And you want to be able to do your own washing without going a hundred miles off campus. The washing machines up there were horrible. I didn't actually use them. I brought my washing home.' Initially, Emily went home every Friday and returned every Sunday, which was what most of the people along her corridor did. However, as time passed, a sense of community developed: 'We established a mealtime and everyone went into the kitchen at about 6 to start cooking and we were in the kitchen from 6 until about 8 at night. And everyone literally went in there so it felt like being at home with the family. We did our own, but we did proper meals. Every Wednesday we went to Burger King. But generally speaking we cooked our own stuff. However, those that lived closer to the Burger Kings, the fish and chip shops, the pizza places, did have a lot of take-out food and ready meals.' As she settled in, Emily's visits home became less frequent, and she now goes home one weekend in four. In her second year, she found a flat through an estate agency and shared it with three other women from her original corridor.

The academic side of life soon fell into place. Emily was pleasantly surprised by the accessibility of staff and their willingness to help with problems. She is an organised person who has been able to plan her time well and deliver all her assignments on schedule. For Emily, the only downside to university life is the financial cost. Her parents pay her tuition fees and she has a loan which she tops up by working throughout every holiday in a restaurant near her home. She is very careful with money and thinks she will leave with debts of £9,000. The likelihood that she will obtain a teaching post immediately after graduation softens the blow considerably: 'That is what reassures me that I will be alright. I've got something there at the end.'

▶ Conor

Conor opted for a foundation degree.
Conor is in his first year of a two-year foundation degree in IT for E-Business. Now aged 38, he admits: 'This is the first time I have been back to academic education since I left school some 20 years ago, so this is a new/fresh challenge for me. This is also the reason why I chose a Foundation Degree over a BSc, as I was unsure whether I could adapt to the academic environment after so many years.'

Conor holds 'an IT Team Leader's position within a large global banking organisation, managing a team of six operational staff. The team works shifts delivering services 24 hours a day, 365 days a year.' His employers pay 60 per cent of his tuition fees and he is paid for a full week although he spends Wednesdays at university. However, in return, he is prepared to work through his lunch hours on other days and go in on Saturdays if necessary. His employers also benefit directly from some of the work-based projects undertaken as part of Conor's degree, such as customised web-page design.

He chose this particular foundation degree because it 'covered a wide range of modules that I felt would be useful in moving within different IT specific areas, both within my organisation and externally. This includes programming, web design and networking.' In addition, the 'option to top-up to an Honours degree after completing the Foundation Degree. Honours provided an additional goal to focus on.' Moreover it was logistically possible as the degree requires attendance at college for lectures 'one day a week (09:30–19:30). Whilst this is a long day, it was easier to persuade the company to give me a day off a week to do this degree, then to try and ask for two or maybe three half days.'

Conor believes that his course 'is an excellent foundation for those individuals who are unsure whether to undertake an Honours Degree. It can in many ways give them the confidence to progress their education further. It is by far the best stepping stone for individuals who have not undertaken any academic education for some years. The foundation degree in E-Business (generic route) is designed specifically to provide a valuable combination of wide-ranging technical and business skills alongside academic knowledge, whilst enabling an individual to focus in the latter stages on a variety of specialisms. This will also include opportunities to acquire a vendor's qualification for CISCO, something that is used within the company's IT network infrastructure.'

'This course will equip me in describing and applying system analysis and design methodologies to e-business projects, to assembling data and producing complex documents, to understanding computer architecture, operating systems, data bases in addition to providing a framework for the comparison of fundamental elements of programming languages. This particular IT degree offers me the opportunity to build on an extensive history of work experiences gained within my organisation. I believe that its focus on practicality and industry needs alongside academic progression is an ideal combination for an IT professional such as myself.'

'Balancing work, studying and family life and my passion for golf will be challenging over the next two years, especially whilst continuing to work unsociable hours, seven days a week. It will be important to get the support from within my family as well as my colleagues within my workplace. Overall the thought of studying again hasn't been as daunting as first felt, which is probably why I have settled in so well. I still have reservations as to whether I would still be able to balance this with everything else in my life as the course progresses. We will just have to wait and see and take each day as it comes.'

▶ Natasha

At 25, Natasha is considered to be a mature student. She is married with two sons aged 5 and 18 months.

'When I was younger I continued at school into the sixth form, I contracted glandular fever at 16 and missed a lot of work. This and the fact I was very unhappy at the school contributed to me leaving before finishing my A-levels in Sociology and Theatre Studies. I then took a training programme placement at xxx Airlines, Heathrow, for six months which was fantastic. It gave me my first taste of the real world and made me realise that people much more accomplished and older than me found my abilities impressive and my company interesting. After this I decided to go back to college and take A-levels. However, soon after starting the course I met my now husband and fell absolutely head over heels. There were many places I preferred being at that time than college and I didn't return the second year. I was then surprisingly thrown head first into the real world in a different sense because I fell pregnant, with our eldest son. Absolutely the best thing that has ever happened to me! I grew up extremely quickly and have been devoted since that moment to being as good a parent as I possibly can be. Over the last five years I have been a mother primarily. I have had a few part-time office jobs and bar jobs, keeping myself interactive with the working world and the money enough to keep our heads above water. Now I have found myself wanting to start the journey of finding my career path desperately.'

'I heard about the course thanks to my mum, who noted that it wasn't necessary for mature students to have A-levels. I went along [to the open day] and talked to people running courses, trying to find out how I could apply. I had a brief meeting that day with the department head, and outlined to her my interests and ambitions in life.'

'So, well, now I am at uni [first-year media studies with creative writing and video production] 11 hours a week for lectures and seminars, more if I have group assignments that need discussion and research. My mother-in-law mainly looks after my youngest while I am at college, but he has just started going to a local nursery one day a week which luckily is funded through my LEA. I work in a pub, 12 hours a week, for now . . . soon I am changing my shifts and dropping one every fortnight, to give a breather in my diary. The rest of the time I do school runs, cook, clean, spend time with my kids, and spend most evenings either reading or sat in front of my computer keeping up to date with my work. I am extremely busy, but I am loving every second of it.'

'I have felt different from other students in some respects . . . I haven't yet really socialised with anyone (other than quick coffees in the union bar in between seminars) but I have made some good friends even on that basis. Most of the people I have met since first starting found it hard to believe I was 25 . . . I look younger as everyone tells me (and have braces on my teeth which also helps that!!), let alone married and with two children . . . at first I think they weren't sure if I would act a lot older than them, but soon realised that that wasn't the case. I have a more mature outlook and unlike most of them always am up to date with the work, probably due to my emotional maturity being such a must in my everyday life, but I still have a lot in common with them because our interests and talents are similar.'

'As far I am concerned, my mind and my life has been opened up in a way I have felt for a long time it was meant to be and needed to be. My children are very happy, bright young things who I still feel get absolutely enough of my time for them. My parents, friends and everyone else who knows me through uni or work, seem very happy for me and alot of the time in awe of how much I do. I myself am very proud of myself for doing something about getting to where I want to go. Because as cocky as it may sound I really believe I have something to give creatively, and I would have gone mad not being able to use it or reach for the sky as I intend to continue doing.'

▶ John

John is in his first year, studying mechanical engineering, having secured his place through the clearing process.

'I chose my course by looking at what I was good at and what I enjoy, and that meant engineering as I found the theories and possibility of practical work a great attraction to the course I wanted to do. When I was choosing my universities I used the league tables and UCAS books available to me to look at the courses that I had the grades for and slightly above, and from this then picked a short list and did further research on each as to how other areas of the university were – not just the academic [side] – things like the geographical position and extracurricular activities.'

'As I had to go through clearing and into a university I did not have time to research deeply or take a look around properly, I was very unsure what to expect. When I got here what I found was that it was actually smaller than I thought it would be. [I thought there would be] about 13,000 students and then in fresher's week there only being a couple of thousand people it made it feel quite empty, and in some ways like quite a close community as you kept seeing people that you recognised.'

'As I came through clearing I didn't get any choice [about where to live]. I was more worried about just getting accommodation which meant that I ended up in the least desirable halls, but I found that they were fine and that I didn't need my own bathroom – just a room to sleep in and the kitchen to chill in. So even though I had no choice it worked out well and it would have been very hard for it to work out better.'

'The worst thing about leaving home was the feeling that you had forgotten something while you were driving up the motorway. The worst thing is realising that you have left something and do have to go back to get it. Also, having to do everything for yourself is a great experience, being completely independent. I didn't have any real feelings about it except for the freedom.'

'Making out a budget was relatively easy. Sticking to it is a completely different thing, especially during the first couple of weeks where there are always loads of opportunities to spend a little extra on other supplies that you don't really need. Not to mention the essentials that you had never before thought of buying like a TV licence or washing-up liquid. It's also a weird feeling being in debt for the first time and starting your overdraft.'

'The differences I found between studying at university and studying at school is mainly the class size – from classes of 10–15 to classes of 150 is an interesting transition. [Also], the expectation that you will take the initiative and do the work even when you are not told to do it and never chased up about it. Be careful to try not to get too bored with your course – sometimes you need to persevere with some of the repetition of A-level work as this can [otherwise] lead down a bad road of missing lectures and then missing important information which will lead to ultimate failure!'

'To fit in socially, be yourself and get involved, even if the first people you meet are not your kind of people or you are not their kind of person, you will meet someone you get on with, and then everything will fit. You find such a diversity of people at university, there is always someone you will get on with.'

▶ Linda

Linda opted for distance learning, so that she could take full-time paid employment and avoid debt.

Linda is a distance learning student, currently in the third year of her BA Honours in Business Studies and Law. She is 20 years old and lives with her boyfriend, who is a student at a 'conventional' university. She works full-time as an administrator in a solicitor's office and uses the hour-long train journey to and from work as an opportunity to study. In addition to this she devotes part of every weekend to tackling the reading lists associated with her course, and does some 'lighter' work, such as drawing diagrams, in her office lunch hours. She confirms: 'I enjoy what I study so I don't look upon it as doing too much work or as a chore. I enjoy what I read.'

Linda believes that there are many advantages to combining distance learning with paid employment. She recalls: 'I have always been a very independent learner and when it came to the decision about whether to attend 'conventional' university the choice was very simple for me. With all the changes my year group faced with the university system and the loans that were introduced to replace the grant system, I felt that 'conventional' university did not appeal to me. With the choice that I have taken, I have been able to get a good full-time job so that I am earning a good wage and gaining on-the-job experience at the same time as doing a degree. I will not have the debt at the end of my degree like my school friends and will also have the equivalent years in experience . . . I believe you have to be more committed if you study through the xxx university [distance learning institution] as it is true that you do not always feel like studying when you get in from work at 7.30 p.m. However, knowing that I am taking a harder route to achieve my degree and that I will gain more out of it by the end, by not having huge debts and instead having the equivalent years' experience, keeps me motivated.'

Linda is somewhat irritated by comments from others that distance learning automatically involves missing out on student life. She meets other students from her institution frequently in pubs and cafés and has two particular local friends with whom she has enjoyed outings such as bowling evenings over the past two years: 'I do not feel like I have missed out socially by not attending a full-time university, as the xxx university has so many social events as well as having face-to-face tutorials and interactive online conferences. Personally I do not feel that 'student life' of wild parties and late-night drinking is what I would have gone to university for. I would have gone purely to do a degree. An example I have recently come across regarding the balance of time between work and socialising for students is that a friend who attends xxx university failed his second-year resit exams after failing the initial ones, due to spending more time socialising than doing the work. Consequently he now has to wait until the summer to retake those exams before continuing with the third year of his course. This has put him a whole year behind.'

In summary, Linda is proud of choosing distance learning and hopes that 'my commitment to my studies whilst doing a full-time job will reflect on my personality to prospective employers in the future'.

11 Checklists

▶ Have You Decided on Your Course?

If so, turn to the next page. If not, consider the following options:

- ▶ Think about what you enjoy most and where your talents lie.

- ▶ Ask for guidance from your careers tutor or a member of staff who knows you well.

- ▶ Take the Stamford Test, designed to match your interests, ambitions and skills to subject areas (available on www.ucas.ac.uk).

- ▶ Think about what you want to do after university and check out the qualifications required.

- ▶ Look at the details of destinations of higher education leavers (contact the university in question and look at the information on www.hesa.ac.uk). Ensure that others have entered your chosen profession having completed the course you are considering taking.

- ▶ Once you have narrowed your choice a little, look at the specific information available on www.ucas.ac.uk and www.aimhigher.ac.uk.

- ▶ Check out the profiles of institutions in which you may be interested on www.educationguardian.co.uk.

- ▶ Check out the quality of courses, curriculum design, learning resources, modes of assessment etc. on www.qaa.ac.uk.

- ▶ Does the course generally have a good reputation?

- ▶ Check out websites and open days before finally making your choice.

► Have You Decided on Your Shortlist of Institutions?

If so, turn to the next page. If you have decided on your course but not where you want to study it, consider the following before making your choice:

- ► Do you want to study full-time or part time?

- ► Do you want to live at home while you are studying?

- ► Is distance learning an option that would suit you?

- ► Do you want to be within a certain distance of home?

- ► Are good public transport links important, either for a specific journey or in general?

- ► Do you have strong views about living in an urban or a rural environment?

- ► Would you prefer a campus environment or not?

- ► Do you think a large university or a small one would suit you better?

- ► Do you have any special requirements, e.g. crèche facilities?

- ► Living costs vary from area to area. Does this affect your shortlist?

- ► Is there enough/too much nightlife?

- ► What are your chances of getting university accommodation and what are the options if you don't?

- ► Check out websites and open days before finally making your choice.

► Checklist of What to Do before Going to University

Finance

- ► Apply for your student loan and any other student support (forms are available from your LEA or equivalent or online – see Chapter 5).
- ► Set up a bank account if you don't already have one. Some people

prefer to have two (one for week-to-week expenses and the other for large amounts such as loan payments).

► Work out a budget in advance.

► Set up any necessary direct debits.

Accommodation

► Find somewhere to live. Your first port of call is the university accommodation office. Ask about all the possibilities – halls of residence, student flats, private-sector halls, hostels, private rentals and lodgings. If you are renting privately, refer back to the information in Chapter 6 regarding your rights and what to look for when you view a property. If the university cannot help you, order the local paper in advance and sign on with local agents to ensure that you will find somewhere before term starts.

► Get a TV licence if you intend to take a TV.

► Organise insurance for your possessions.

► Sign up with the utility companies if appropriate.

Acquire lifestyle skills

► Ensure that you know how to use a washing machine and iron and that you understand laundry instructions.

► Check which cleaning products to use for various tasks.

► Ensure that you have a basic knowledge of what things cost, especially food.

► Practise a few easy recipes before you leave.

► Practise living on a budget and keeping note of your expenditure.

► Create a file for all your administrative matters at university.

► Try some basic maintenance, e.g. changing a fuse.

▶ Checklist of What to Take to University

Clothes

▶ Whatever you want to wear, bearing in mind you will have to launder your own clothes. Remember a warm, waterproof coat and comfortable walking shoes.

Hobbies

▶ Anything you need to pursue your hobbies such as sports equipment and clothing.

Studying

▶ A computer and printer if you have them; spare disks; stationery; books from your course booklist and any useful college or A-level books. A student diary or planner will also be useful.

Paid work

▶ If you intend to work somewhere that has a particular dress code, for example a smart restaurant, take the appropriate clothes and shoes with you. Also any relevant references and a copy of your CV.

Cooking

▶ Ask the accommodation office or your landlord what is available and what you will need to provide. See Chapter 3 for a list of basic utensils, crockery, cutlery and food. Don't forget tea/coffee and biscuits for the first day.

Cleaning

▶ A couple of cleaning cloths and any specific products that you may need for your room/flat.

Your room

▶ In order to personalise your room you may wish to bring posters, rugs, photos, music etc.

Paperwork

▶ Take a file for all your paperwork. Use dividers to keep everything in order. In this file you should keep: your bank details; loan details; insurance details; national insurance card; NHS card if you have one; correspondence with your tax office if appropriate; spare copies of your CV and references; spare passport photos. You should also include your correspondence with the university, although this may require a second file.

Miscellaneous
- ▶ Your personal address book
- ▶ Mobile phone
- ▶ Bank cards; cheque book; passport.

▶ What to Do in the First Few Days at University

- ▶ Register with your department, and faculty too if necessary.

- ▶ Ensure that there are no problems with your student loan arrangements. If the money has not arrived, contact the Student Loans Company helpline on Freephone 0800 40 50 10, Monday to Friday, from 9.00 a.m. to 5.30 p.m.

- ▶ Pay any necessary fees such as tuition fees and hall fees.

- ▶ Obtain your students' union card and information about the benefits of being a member.

- ▶ Get a library card; acquaint yourself with the library hours, layout and procedure, and sign up for a library tour if appropriate.

- ▶ Register with a GP and a dentist, plus an optician if appropriate.

- ▶ Get to know the campus/local area. Check out the nearest good place to shop, note interesting pubs and bars, and the nearest bus stops and bus routes.

- ▶ Organise your room so that you can live and work in it, and find what you need easily.

- ▶ Establish where to go for lectures and seminars and generally start to get to know your new location.

- ▶ Acquire all the timetables and core books you need to get started, and make a note of the date by which you have to select which modules to take.

▶ Make sure you have the stationery you require for your studies.

▶ Read through all the information you have been sent about Freshers' Week to make sure that you don't miss anything good.

▶ Make sure that you have the necessary things in your room to be able to offer your new flatmates tea, coffee or a drink, as this is a good way to get to know your neighbours.

▶ If you want to find a part-time job, buy and read the local paper and/or pop into local bars, restaurants etc. to ask if there are any vacancies.

▶ Join at least one society as it's a good way to make friends.

▶ Accept *all* invitations while you find your feet.

▶ Ten Top Tips for Getting the Most out of Your Time at University

▶ Give yourself time to settle in. It can take a surprisingly long while before you feel absolutely comfortable with your new life. If you are still feeling unhappy or unsettled after the first few months, or at any later time during your undergraduate years, don't keep your feelings to yourself. Talk to your friends, a student counsellor or your GP, or contact Nightline or the Samaritans.

▶ Each new semester, write out a personal timetable which includes any employment commitments, scheduled study such as lectures, at least one library session per week, private study, planned activities such as clubs and societies, and time for rest and relaxation with your friends. Try to stick to it in principle.

▶ Make sure that you attend all your lectures, seminars and tutorials, even if you have not had time to do the background reading. It will help you to form an impression of the broader picture.

▶ Back up all important work and keep the disk apart from your computer, in a safe place.

▶ Take advantage of some of the opportunities afforded by university life by learning new activities through clubs and societies or by participating in exchange programmes.

▶ If your budget is not working out, ask for help. In fact, if you find you are not coping with finances, work or any other aspect of student life, seek help as soon as possible. Advisers have generally seen all the problems before and can usually find a strategy to deal with them.

▶ Remember that you need to sleep and don't be tempted to skip meals. If you are very busy, make sure that you have emergency food supplies to hand and keep healthy snacks in your room, such as fruit.

▶ If you are unwell, seek medical advice. It is better to be safe than sorry, especially when there is a risk of outbreaks of mumps and meningitis amongst students.

▶ If you are planning a late night out, make sure that you are with other people and that you won't have to get home alone.

▶ Ensure that you have enough time with your friends, as if there are bad times, having good friends will help you through. Friends are one of the best aspects of student life!

Good luck!

**Enjoy university
and the student life
experience.**

Appendix

Useful Websites and Telephone Numbers

► **General Student Websites**

www.educationguardian.co.uk	For news and information on higher education courses
www.missyourmum.com	Contains lots of student advice including meals on a budget, finance, accommodation, and health and safety
www.nistudents.org	The student movement in Northern Ireland
www.nusonline.co.uk	National Union of Students (NUS); gives general advice for students as well as information about the work of the NUS and current campaigns
www.opendays.com	University and college open day directory
www.studentfreestuff.com	Freebies for students
www.universityoptions.co.uk	Contains advice and information on making the move into higher education

► **Government Websites**

www.aimhigher.ac.uk	Aimhigher; provides useful information on higher education, e.g. courses and student loans
www.delni.gov.uk	The Department for Employment and Learning Northern Ireland
www.dfes.gov.uk/studentsupport/	The Higher Education Student Support website
www.dh.gov.uk	Department of Health
www.fco.gov.uk	The Foreign and Commonwealth Office
www.hesa.ac.uk	The Higher Education Statistics Agency (HESA)

www.hse.gov.uk	Health and Safety Executive
www.inlandrevenue.gov.uk	Inland Revenue
www.learning.wales.gov.uk or www.dysgu.cymru.gov.uk	The Welsh Assembly Government's Training and Education website
www.oft.gov.uk Tel. 08457 22 44 99	The Office of Fair Trading
www.qaa.ac.uk	The Quality Assurance Agency for Higher Education (QAA)
www.saas.gov.uk	The Student Awards Agency for Scotland (SAAS)
www.ucas.ac.uk	University and College Admissions Service (UCAS)

▶ Accommodation

www.accommodationforstudents.com	General advice and a directory of student accommodation in the UK
www.arla.co.uk	The Association of Residential Letting Agents
www.bunk.com	Student accommodation in the UK
www.citizensadvice.org.uk	Citizen's Advice Bureau
www.endsleigh.co.uk Tel. 0800 028 3571	Endsleigh; specialises in insurance for students
www.oft.gov.uk Tel. 08457 22 44 99	The Office of Fair Trading; publishes guidance on tenancy agreements
www.shelter.org.uk Tel. 0808 800444	Shelter; advice and help on accommodation issues
www.student-accom.com	Rented accommodation and houses for students
www.tv-l.co.uk	For TV licensing rules and regulations
www.unipol.leeds.ac.uk/largercode/	For students considering taking up a place in a private hall

▶ Career Guidance

www.drjob.co.uk	Advice and jobs for graduates
www.gradunet.co.uk	Careers advice and job finder for graduates
www.hobsons.com	Guidance and jobs for school leaves and graduates

www.insidecareers.co.uk	Career advice and graduate vacancies
www.prospects.ac.uk	Official graduate careers website

▶ Disability

www.bda-dyslexia.org.uk	The British Dyslexia Association
www.disability.gov.uk	Government's disability issues site
www.drc-gb.org	Disability Rights Commission
www.futurenet.co.uk/charity/ado/adomenu	Adult dyslexia organisation; offers support and advice for students
www.hefce.ac.uk	Higher Education Funding Council for England; includes a resource directory for disabilities
www.skill.org.uk	National bureau to support students with disabilities

▶ Employment

www.adviceguide.org	Employment rights advice from the Citizens Advice Bureau
www.cre.gov.uk	Commission for Racial Equality
www.emplaw.co.uk	Information on British employment law
www.hse.gov.uk	Health and Safety Executive
www.inlandrevenue.gov.uk	Provides details on tax and national insurance payments
www.i-resign.com/uk/home	Leaving your job
www.morethanwork.net	Employment advice for working students
www.ukcosa.org.uk	Includes advice on working for international students

▶ Finance

www.adviceguide.org.uk	Finance advice from the Citizen Advice Bureau
www.aimhigher.ac.uk	Aimhigher includes information on student finance
www.britishcouncil.org	British Council; includes guidance on student finance
www.cccs.co.uk	Consumer Credit Counselling Service (CCCS), which includes the Student Debtline

www.delni.gov.uk	The Department for Employment and Learning Northern Ireland
www.dfes.gov.uk/studentsupport/	The Higher Education Student Support website
www.hothouses.com	A database of educational opportunities including sponsorship and scholarships
www.inlandrevenue.gov.uk/taxcredits Tel. 0800 500 222	For Child Tax Credits from the Inland Revenue
www.learning.wales.gov.uk or www.dysgu.cymru.gov.uk	The Welsh Assembly Government's Training and Education website
www.nationaldebtline.co.uk Tel. 0808 808 4000	National Debtline; provides advice on how to deal with debt problems
www.nusonline.co.uk	Includes guidance on student finance
www.saas.gov.uk	The Student Awards Agency for Scotland (SAAS)
www.slc.co.uk	The Student Loans Company
Student Debtline	Tel. 0800 328 1813
www.switchwithwhich.co.uk or www.moneysupermarket.com	For finding good finance deals

▶ Health, Safety and Security

www.studenthealth.co.uk	Good health advice for students, written by doctors
www.nutrition.org.uk	The British Nutrition Foundation; offers many suggestions for healthy eating
www.eatwell.gov.uk	The Food Standards Agency; includes information on healthy eating and food hygiene
www.dh.gov.uk	Department of Health
www.hse.gov.uk	Health and Safety Executive
www.nhsdirect.nhs.uk Tel. 0845 46 47	NHS Direct
www.travelhealth.co.uk	Health advice for travelling abroad
www.ppa.org.uk Tel. 0845 850 1166	The Prescription Pricing Authority
www.brook.org.uk	Brook; provides free and confidential sexual health advice and contraception for young people

www.fpa.org.uk
Tel. 0845 310 1334 (UK),
0141 576 5088 (Scotland),
028 90 325 488 (Belfast) or
028 71 260 016 (Derry)

The Family Planning Association; offers advice on a range of sexual health issues

www.bpas.org
Tel. 08457 30 40 30 (UK),
44 121 450 7700 (from Ireland)

British Pregnancy Advisory Service

www.mariestopes.org.uk
Tel. 0845 300 80 90

Marie Stopes Clinics; offers advice on sexual health issues

www.playingsafely.co.uk
Tel. 0800 567 123 (UK),
Tel. 0845 604 8484 (Wales)

Sexual health line

www.tht.org.uk
Tel. 0845 1221 200

The Terrence Higgins Trust; for information and advice on HIV/AIDS and good sexual health

www.rapecrisis.org.uk

For information and details of rape crisis centres across the UK

www.roofie.com
Tel. 0800 783 2980

The Roofie Foundation; an advisory centre for victims of drug-related rape and sexual abuse

www.samaritans.org.uk
Tel. 08457 90 90 90 (UK),
1850 60 90 90 (Republic of Ireland)

The Samaritans is a confidential 24-hour helpline for anyone in crisis

www.nightline.niss.ac.uk

Nightline is a confidential helpline run by students for students

www.helplines.org.uk

Telephone Helplines Association

www.queery.org.uk
Tel. 020 7837 7324

Lesbian, gay, bisexual and transexual life

www.stonewall.org.uk

Equality and justice for lesbians, gay men and bisexuals

www.alcoholconcern.org.uk
Tel. 0207 928 7377

Alcohol Concern is the national agency on alcohol misuse

www.givingupsmoking.co.uk
Tel. 0800 169 0169

NHS Smoking Helpline

www.ash.org.uk
Tel. 020 7739 5902

ASH (Action on Smoking and Health)

www.quit.org.uk
Tel. 0800 00 22 00

Quit; for help on giving up smoking

www.talktofrank.com
Tel. 0800 77 66 00
Textphone: 0800 917 8765

National Drugs Helpline/Talk to Frank; offers confidential advice on drug-related issues

www.knowthescore.info
Tel. 0800 587 5789

Know the Score; drugs helpline for Scotland

www.endsleigh.co.uk
Tel. 0800 028 3571

Endsleigh; specialises in insurance for students

www.immobilise.com

Advice on mobile phone crime

www.secureyourmotor.gov.uk

Advice on securing your vehicle

www.suzylamplugh.org

The Suzy Lamplugh Trust is a leading authority on personal safety

www.victimsupport.org.uk
Tel. 0845 30 30 900

Victim Support, helps people cope with the effects of crime

► **International Students**

www.britishcouncil.org

British Council; includes guidance on student finance

www.cisuk.org.uk

Council for International Students. CISUK is a national organisation set up and run by student representatives to promote the interests of international students studying in the UK

www.educationuk.org

Produced by the British Council to help international students interested in a UK course or qualification.

www.ukcosa.org.uk

Includes useful general advice for international students studying in the UK

► **Study Skills and PDP**

www.skills4study.com

Guidance on study skills and personal development planning (PDP)

► **Travel**

www.fco.gov.uk
Tel. 0870 606 0290

Travel advice from the Foreign and Commonwealth Office

www.istc.org

International Student Travel Confederation

www.nationalexpress.com

National Express website

www.railcard.co.uk

National Railcard website

www.raileurope.co.uk

Specialists in European rail travel

www.roughguides.co.uk
and www.letsgo.com

Travel guides

www.statravel.co.uk	Discount travel for students
www.travelhealth.co.uk	Health advice for travellers
www.yha.org.uk	International Youth Hostels Association

Notes

1. Organization for Economic Co-operation and Development.
2. DfES, *Higher Education Funding – International Comparisons*, January 2004.
3. Prime Minister's Press Conference, 15 January 2004.
4. See, for example, 'VCs "warned" about top-up fee failings', *Guardian*, 21 September 2004.
5. As above.
6. University of Oxford, *Oxford's Academic Strategy: A Green Paper*, January 2005, paragraphs 62 and 63.
7. As above, paragraph 93.
8. As above, paragraph 95.
9. Rebecca Smithers, 'Oxford may slash number of British students to cut debt', *Guardian*, 25 January 2005.
10. Sarah Harris, 'Oxford under fire over its cuts in British students', *Daily Mail*, 26 January 2005.
11. See, for example, Rebecca Smithers, 'Science department closures threaten medicine, warns BMA', *Guardian*, 23 December 2004.
12. *The UNITE 'Student Experience Report', 2005*. The survey was carried out by MORI on behalf of the UNITE group. The report was also conducted in association with HEPI (Higher Education Policy Institute). This quotation is from a press release, *Higher Education Students Come Clean*, 25 January 2005.
13. Quoted in 'Fees to triple student debt, says report', *Guardian*, 28 January 2005.
14. Department for Education and Skills, *The Future of Higher Education*, Cm 5735, January 2003, paragraph 6.1.
15. HESA, press release PR78, *2002/03 Performance Indicators Published*, 30 September 2004.
16. House of Commons Education and Skills Committee, *The Future of Higher Education. Fifth Report of the Session 2002–3* (July 2003), conclusions and recommendations, points 22–5.
17. Department for Education and Skills, *Widening Participation in Higher Education* (2003).

18. Professor Steven Schwartz (Chair), *Fair Admissions to Higher Education: Recommendations for Good Practice* (September 2004).
19. As above, section 4.3.
20. Rebecca Smithers, 'Clarke fuels row over university access', *Guardian*, 26 February 2003.
21. 'Edinburgh to lower grades for state school pupils', *Guardian*, 18 February 2003.
22. Donald MacLeod, 'New friends in the north', *Guardian*, 4 February 2003.
23. Bahram Bekhradnia, Higher Education Policy Institute, *Widening Participation and Fair Access: An Overview of the Evidence* (February 2003), Executive Summary 19–20.
24. Prime Minister's Press Conference, 15 January 2004.
25. Data from OECD, *Education at a Glance 2002* (2001 data published in 2002), cited in DfES, *Higher Education Funding – International Comparisons*, January 2004.
26. MacLeod, 'New friends in the north'.
27. Quoted in Laura Clark, '£420 million, That's the annual cost to taxpayers from students dropping out of degree courses', *Daily Mail*, 18 January 2005.
28. Polly Curtis, '"Open access" universities policy backfires', *Guardian*, 17 January 2005.
29. Higher Education Statistics Agency, Press release PR78, 30 September 2004.
30. See, for example, Sarah Harris, 'Ex-poly universities hit by student dropout crisis', *Daily Mail*, 30 September 2004.
31. Rebecca Smith, 'Middlesex to abolish first-year exams', *Guardian*, 15 October 2004.
32. Quoted in Curtis, '"Open access" universities policy backfires'.
33. *The UNITE 'Student Experience Report'*, 2005. This quotation is from a press release, *Higher Education Students Come Clean*, 25 January 2005.
34. As above.
35. Association of Graduate Recruiters, press release, *Employers Report the Biggest Increase in Graduate Vacancies since 2000*, 14 July 2004.
36. Median figures given.
37. Graduate Prospects, press release, *Graduates Set for a Happy New Year as Salaries Exceed 20k*, 6 January 2005.
38. HESA press release, PR80, *72.7 per cent of Full-time Leavers Enter Employment*, 2 November 2004.
39. Matthew Taylor, 'Research reveals harsh reality of life after college', *Guardian*, 3 January 2005.
40. Peter Elias and Kate Purcell, *Seven Years On: Graduate Careers in a*

Changing Labour Market, funded by the ESRC (Economic and Social Research Council) and HECSU (Higher Education Careers Services Unit). Press release, 16 June 2004.

41. Quoted in Graduate Prospects press release, *Maths Graduates are Good News for Teaching*, 21 January 2005.
42. Information from nusonline.co.uk.
43. Figures from the DfES.
44. DfES, *A Guide to Financial Support for Higher Education Students in 2005/2006*, p. 46.
45. 2005/6 figures from www.inlandrevenue.gov.uk .
46. Stella Cottrell, *The Palgrave Student Planner* (Basingstoke: Palgrave Macmillan, 2005).
47. Stella Cottrell, *The Study Skills Handbook*, 2nd edition (Basingstoke: Palgrave Macmillan, 2003).
48. *Students' Access to Healthcare*, NUS web-based survey undertaken between September to December 2003 involving 1689 valid responses..
49. NHS, *Alcohol: Facts for Young People*, 2000.
50. NHS, *Need Help Giving Up Smoking?*, November 2002.
51. See www.nusonline.co.uk (section on food safety within 'health').
52. See Home Office website www.good2bsecure.gov.uk.
53. Open University, *OU Increasingly Attractive to Younger Students*, press release PR4767, 14 November 2003.
54. The British Council, *Feeling at Home*, 2002, p. 13.
55. As above, p. 4.

Index